Enhancing Study Skills
for a Successful Degree

Farhat A. Hussain

Historian, Archaeologist, Explorer, Sociologist, Educationalist.
(London, Exeter, Cambridge, Edinburgh, Manchester, Durham.)

Enhancing study skills for a successful degree
ISBN: 978-0-9555432-0-3
Published by *The Knowledge and Skills Foundation*

www.knowledgeskills.org

Text and illustrations by Farhat A. Hussain
Copyright © 2007 Farhat A. Hussain
All rights reserved

The right of Farhat A. Hussain to be identified as author of this work has been asserted by him in accordance with the Copyright, Designs and Patents Act 1988.

No part of this publication may be reproduced, stored in a retrieval system, or transmitted in any form or by any means, electronic, mechanical, photocopying, recording or otherwise, without the prior permission of the Publishers and author.

- so there is adequate time to focus more upon exam preparation.
- Add more quotations and references to your exam prep notes. Fine tune & advance your analysis. Practice answering exam questions from past papers. Discuss with peers and tutors.

- Stay fit and healthy
- Maintain focus
- Maintain motivation

Allocate adequate time each week such as a specific study session for exam preparation. Focus on what required of you in the exams and what areas you must address. Familiarise yourself with topics, issues, debates, analysis, quotations. Read from various sources of books ans and journals. Discuss your reading with peers and tutors.

Whilst ascertaining course requirements, undertaking reading and coursework, ensure you have a clear picture as to exam dates, structure and requirements of examinations and begin preparations for exams (whether exams take place at end of first term or end of academic year). Obtain past papers, ensure your studies and your examination preparation compliment one another.

- both course notes and exam prep notes.
- before final term/semester
- Second term/semester
- First term
- During break ensure you go over work from first term

Start of academic year **First term/semester**

Whilst breakdown of academic year in this diagram is based upon the UK university organisation of three terms the basic princples on this diagram may be applied at comparative periods in the year to any university in any country.

© Farhat A. Hussain 2007

Enhancing Study Skills

Examination Preparation for end of year examinations

www.knowledgeskills.org

Go through all your work in an orderly and scholarly manner Ensure your work flows through your mind.

Ask your tutor for time to discuss your exam preparation clarify what you have covered and seek advice as to any potential areas of weakness.

Maximise time spent on exam preparation cut down on many other activities by this time.

Go through course and exam prep notes. Ensure you have mastery of major debates and issues and you are able to write comprehensively with authority with clear analysis and sound conclusions based upon analysis of evidence.

Final term/ semester

Place exam dates into your schedule

Examinations

Be clear, comprehensive yet concise, be orderly, use evidence, analysis, firm conclusions, be calm!

Maintain focus
Maintain concentration
Maintain understanding

Enjoy a well deserved break

Preface

University studies represent one of the most challenging, rewarding and significant periods of a person's life and impact significantly upon the future of a student. It is essential to enjoy the privilege of life as a university student yet as a university student you must never lose sight as to why you are at university. It is essential for university students to perform well in studies in order to secure a successful future. Successful university studies require far more than subject knowledge. University degrees are conferred on the basis of secure subject knowledge that has been demonstrated via the undertaking of comprehensive studies that involve the application and mastery of a range of key study skills such as methodology, interpretation and analysis. Study skills are essential tools for success at university.

A number of strategies may be considered and implemented with a view to successful studies and success in life at this crucial time. Successful studying must be undertaken in conjunction with successful living as the two possess a symbiotic relationship and the former cannot be effectively achieved at the detriment to the latter.

This piece of work is designed to provide readers an insight into what constitutes key study skills and how to enhance study skills which are vital tools for successful study undergraduate level at university and will serve of use to readers in postgraduate studies and in subsequent work and life. This work is sub-divided into a range of areas, each of which is of prime significance in its own right. Whilst written in reference to university study in the UK (though the writer has undertaken courses in European and International systems and practice of education and lectures at a number of universities in various countries across the world each year) this piece of work may be applied with equal vigour to those readers who are undertaking their degree studies in North America, the Gulf States, Australia and the other countries that this piece of work will be available in (including China, South Korea, Taiwan, Singapore, Japan, New Zealand, Australia and South Africa).

Due to the nature and scope of this publication each section is dealt with by way of concise introduction. It is hoped that a more detailed edition of this work will be published in the future when time permits. Due to the inter-related nature of topics that comprise enhancing study skills, overlap exists below, where a number of points are valid under a number of headings. Identifying and ascertaining the inter-relationships between phenomenon and knowledge, which includes also that which is required in the acquisition of knowledge, is essential in successful study. The various segments of study skills outlined below are interrelated and form an effective holistic approach to successful study. Where overlap of key concepts and skills occurs this should serve to illustrate the respective point whilst also serving to reinforce the key skill or issue concerned.

This work comprises both text and conceptual charts and diagrams which both serve to aid the reader in respect to understanding and developing study skills for university study. The charts serve to reinforce and develop areas of study skills that are featured (for the most part) in the text as well as to serve as useful guides for study skills in their own right. Whilst each illustration of diagram/chart has been devised by the writer of this work to address a particular branch of study skills in its own right due to the inter-related nature of study skills the charts should be considered in relation to one another (and indeed in relation to the text of this publication on the whole) as they often deal with areas of study skills that are related to one another. Whilst designed to be appealing to the eye as well as the mind these charts must be considered carefully in respect to their content and have been devised for the reader of this work as a useful insight into study skills for degree study at university. The illustrations should be useful for students studying most subject areas at university. Many issues dealt with in this work will be of relevance and usefulness in both, undergraduate and postgraduate studies as well as aspects of work undertaken in various career paths, including in reference to special projects, by readers. Whilst this edition will address core issues in relation to enhancing study skills it is hoped that a subsequent edition of this work will address some of the issues in this first edition in more detail.

For the reference of the reader whilst the writer of this work is engaged in educational and knowledge based endeavour the underlying basis for the compilation of this work has taken place following numerous requests by students of many universities who have requested guidance and assistance in how to enhance their studies from the writer of this work in reference to the experience of the writer of this work in undertaking study of various degrees at various universities and engagement in research projects, academic writing and lecturing at university level. The writer of this work has considered it a great privilege and honour to share some of his years of experience in research and knowledge based work as well as many years of university studies with a view to contribute to the insight of university students into effective methods for enhancing understanding, insight and performance in regard to university studies. The work undertaken specifically into educational studies that pertains to study skills that the writer of this work has also undertaken over the years has also been integrated into this piece of work. It is the hope of the writer of this work that students will find this work to be a useful aid in their university studies. The writer of this work expresses his best wishes for the successful studies, research and careers of readers of this work.

Farhat A. Hussain

Contents

The value and modus of study at degree level	1
Key differences between pre-university college/high-school and university studies	1
Selecting course options	2
Introduction to study skills	2
Oganisational skills	3
Time management, prioritisation and study strategy	4
Motivation: Remaining motivated from registration to graduation and job interview	6
Successful research: Gathering and retention of knowledge	7
Absorbing and attaining the most from lectures	11
Effective note making	12
Enhancing communication: Written and oral	12
Writing a science paper	14
Referencing	14
Bibliography	15
Oral skills	16
Effective analysis	18

Illustrations

Key study skills	19
Prioritise work and time	20
Effective analysis	21
Effective writing	21
Lectures	22
Seminars	23
Writing an essay	24
Effective oral presentation	25
PowerPoint presentation	25
Remain motivated	26
Experiencing difficulty in studies: some suggestions	27
Concentration	28
Remain focused	31
Peer support	32
Books	34
Marking criteria	35
Feedback from tutors	36
Intellectual development	37
Organisational skills	37
Self-reflection	38
Numeracy	39
Respect for others	39

Note making via diagrams	40
Spider diagram	40
Tree diagram	41
Concept mapping	42
The university library	44
Literature review	46
Book/Journal article review	47
Enhancing writing: Elaboration	48
Enhancing writing: Varied grammar	49
Examination preparation	50
Dissertation/Report	50
Health	55
Extra-curricula activities	56
The environment	57
The Author of this work	58

(Text pages continued)

Effective analysis (continued)	59
Problem solving	59
Reading skills	60
Use of the library and the internet	61
Role of tutors	62
Peer support	63
Enhancing participation and performance and deriving benefit in seminars	63
Presentation skills	64
Intellectual development	68
Examination preparation	70
Preparing for a career whilst at university	71
Successful study at home	71
Reflection	72
Dissertation	72
Languages	73
A lifestyle conducive to successful study	74
Opportunities afforded by postgraduate study in relation to learning and career	74
Resources and finance	75
Respect for others	75
Computing literacy	76
International prospects	77
The environment	78
Miscellaneous	80
Endnote	80

The value and modus of study at degree level

Degree level study provides students the means to attain a good standard of education in a particular subject area and also serves as a passport to a career either in the degree subject studied or in a different area (related or wholly different). Degree study provides students the means to attain knowledge and skills that may be applied in work and throughout life and the opportunity to encounter new experiences and expand horizons. Life long friendships are also often formed at university. In regard to a wide range of issues and areas, degree study is a valuable and significant opportunity that must be wholly recognised and appreciated by those reading for a degree. The value and opportunities provided for in reading for a degree must be identified and made good by those engaged in degree study.

Degree level study comprises a range of activity that includes lectures, seminars, reading, written work, exams and much more. Demanding and substantive workload that requires considerable effort and critical analysis, thought and writing characterise study at degree level. In order for students to be successful in their degree studies a knowledge of what is required of students engaged in a degree is essential as is an effective study strategy that contributes to success. Skills attained through effective study strategy and management of one's studies will be of great use and value for both post-graduate study, employment and for one's future on the whole. Reading for a degree is a responsibility for those who have registered for a degree. Students who go to university must adjust their lives so as to ensure adequate time and frame of mind that is conducive and facilitates successful studies is provided for and present throughout the course of the degree. Whilst study skills are essential in pre-university studies, at university study skills are essential tools that will aid effective and successful studies at degree level.

Key differences between pre-university college/high-school and university studies

Whilst the type of pre-university education that 16-18 year olds undergo varies from country to country it is certainly the case that college or high-school education prior to a university degree is far more intense and of higher standard than school study to the age of 16 in all countries. College and high school education is designed to be more rigorous in order to prepare students for university (or employment).

In the United Kingdom, A' (Advanced) levels are amongst the most specialised and high standard courses for the 16-18 age group in the world. Much of the skills of analysis and clear, cohesive, relevant, analytical, critical and concise writing at Advanced (A') level and indeed in respect to college or high school studies in various countries may be used at degree level yet must be built upon as the standard, scope and depth of degree level study is higher than that of A' level/college/high school courses. Degree level study also involves much more workload in terms of reading and coursework as compared to A' level or high school studies. At degree level the emphasis is upon you to do the work in order to succeed – tutors will not spend their careers chasing you up. You either do the work or you do not and, in the case of the latter, you will fail your degree. At degree level in the UK you are essentially reading for the qualification and not listening for it. By way of comparison, at many universities in the USA (the writer of this work has visited and attended lectures at some institutions in North America, communicates with students and members of faculty in North American universities and is aware of degree structures, syllabus, course materials and course requirements of universities in North America) you tend to listen more and are led more by tutors words as compared to degree level study in the UK. In universities across the world degree studies involve a combination of guidance from tutors and initiative and effort by students. At university students must be very aware of what is required of them in respect to attendance at lectures and seminars, undertaking coursework (what work must be undertaken and when it is to be submitted) and preparation for examinations.University studies are far more demanding in scope, level and standard as compared to college or high school level irrespective of which country you may reside in. Whilst many study skills developed at college or high-school will serve as a useful foundation for your degree you must be aware of the nature, scope and depth of university study and develop the particular scope and required level of competence in study skills that are of great use in your university studies irrespective of what subject you will or are studying at university and which country you will or are studying for a university degree in. A good grasp of the composition, purpose and application of study skills for your university studies is essential in ensuring that hard effort in reading, attendance of courses and undertaking coursework and examinations leads to success.

Selecting course options

Degrees comprise a number of courses that are to be taken each year for the duration of the degree. Some degrees allow students to choose a number of course options in addition to compulsory core courses. Select courses that you find to be useful (from your understanding of your degree subject and following consultation with your course tutor), interesting and challenging yet above all, those that you can perform well in. Do not attempt a course that may be too problem-prone for you as this course may serve to be the weak link in your degree. Think carefully about choice of course and do not select a course merely as your friend has decided on this particular course. In many universities it is possible to change your choice of course option within the first week or two of the course. If you feel you would like to change it is essential that you speak to your course tutor and department office as early in the course as possible.

Introduction to Study Skills

Study skills are the tools that students use to ensure that their studies are undertaken effectively and successfully. Students must consider carefully what they are required to undertake as part of their university studies and must plan their time at university accordingly. The day, week, term and year must be planned out well so as to ensure that students gain most from their time. In addition to lectures and seminars, time must be spent in the university library in order to read, absorb and understand the various elements of the degree courses undertaken. Yet in order to ensure that you attain the most from your lectures, seminars and readings and also perform well in your coursework and exams, you must apply study skills throughout your degree. This publication will provide you with an insight into key study skills for university study. Careful attention and application of study skills will contribute to your success at university providing you place a great deal of effort and hard work into your studies and undertake your studies seriously and effectively.

Organisation skills

Being organised is essential in order to achieve success in your studies. Organisational skills provide the means to contribute to successful studies. Whilst there is no absolute universally accepted formula in regard to organisational skills the following elements ought to be integrated into your planning and implementation of studies at university. You must be aware of what your requirements are. Have a clear idea as to what is expected of you for each day of the week of the academic year. Ensure you allocate adequate time to the various tasks you must carry out in the day which will include attending lectures, seminars, getting to and from the lecture theatre or seminar room. Arriving late to seminars and lectures (as well as to appointments with your tutor) is not helpful and will be detrimental to your learning process. Arriving late also creates a bad impression to tutors and to peers and is most disrespectful. Ensure you have allocated adequate time for research and writing in the library and at home.

Maintain a very clear idea of what you need to do and how you will carry out your tasks – the latter should improve with experience providing you are effective in your methodology, your results (including of assignments) will demonstrate if you are succeeding. Writing the main elements of your week in the form of a schedule will help you to plan and undertake your work each day and each week and will aid your organisational effort and ability. It is essential for you to be well versed in what you must undertake. Be realistic in your planning and place effort into the implementation of your work. The sooner you are able to achieve the above the more successful you will become. You must not waste your time on various other pursuits whilst on your course to the extent that you do not bother much to address your studies in an organised, methodical manner or you may fail your degree or may barely pass. It is also essential to maintain a vigilant watch over your overall planner for the academic year. Ensure you have noted down important dates such as submission of course work, appointments to see tutors, examinations and work through the term and year bearing these dates in mind. Be alert as to your requirements and the implementation of what you must undertake, take time into consideration (do not be too slow yet do not rush your work – strike the right balance). Be vigilant as to how you are progressing and constantly consider how you may improve your work and also the organisation of your studies. Put more time into potentially weak areas of your work and seek guidance and help from peers and from tutors.

Spending some time each week discussing study issues and content of work with fellow students or a fellow student will help your understanding of your subject area far more than to work through the academic year by yourself. The academic dialogue you enter into with fellow students will strengthen your insight of the subject and will generate additional ideas and understanding for all concerned. Be aware of time in reference to the day, week, month, term and year (also holiday/break periods). Consider how to maximise on the time that you have. Be organised as outlined above and throughout this publication and also ensure you develop a robust and effective routine in regard to your studies – whether in reference to time spent at university or at home. Effective studies combine time spent at university and at home as addressed in this publication. Also ensure you have a clear idea as to what materials and any other items you may require for your studies and make an effective plan to ensure you have access to what you require such as books, journal articles, software and so forth. Various elements of study skills will help you to be successful in organising your studies effectively such as the ability to undertake research and to write effectively. Ensure your work is also organised effectively (as addressed in this publication). Your work must be methodical, searching, well written, balanced, based upon evidence and comprise effective analysis and conclusion, relevant to the question and of the allocated word length and submitted on time. Ensure your work and your schedule is balanced and effective. Be comfortable and successful. Be in control of your studies. When applied well, organisational skills will help your studies and future work and future life very well. See also below under 'time management' and other related sections of this publication.

Time management, prioritisation and study strategy

You must ensure that you do not waste time during your degree. A few hours wasted each week on irrelevant and useless activity adds up to a massive amount of wasted time over a year and certainly so in relation to a 3-6 year degree. It is essential to be familiar with your schedule of lectures and seminars and to be familiar with how much time you need to spend studying in the library and at home and what work you must submit at what time in the term or semester. A study strategy must be worked out to ensure you succeed in your studies. Your study strategy must involve combining attending lectures and seminars with reading (and making notes) and analysis, discussion with peers, attention to (past) exam papers, tutorials and discussion with your tutor in regard to what your tasks are and suggestions in light of work you are engaged in. Tutors are always happy to help students who demonstrate they are getting on with the work, are interested and respectful of their studies and of their tutor and his/her role. A serious and effective approach to your studies is most conducive to your studies and will result in your tutor writing a much better reference of your work than otherwise will be the case.

Once you are aware of what you must do and have worked out a plan as to how to carry out your tasks each week and for the semester or term and also for the academic year (including when to begin intensive revision), you must, as part of your study strategy, allocate appropriate and effective time to each task. Each day (and night) comprises 24 and not 2400 hours and so you must learn to produce high standard work in good time so that you are free to move on to the next task. Work out what you plan to do each week on a daily basis, around your lectures and seminars and also for the weekends. It is essential to be on top of your work so do not allocate umpteen hours to non-academic pursuits as this will not help your performance and end result. Ensure that your time schedule is realistic and not one that looks impressive on paper yet something you feel you cannot adhere to (in which case your schedule will be useless). Each day should also involve ample rest so that you may recuperate before resuming your work both during the day and at home. Your time schedule should also involve flexibility so that in a day there is, for example, 30 minutes of study time allocated to anything else that needs to be attended to for that day rather than something specific (pre-worked out). In this way, your plan will be more realistic.

It is essential to rapidly come to understand what you need to do in the year, from the start and to work through your requirements as soon as possible so that you have more time in the year rather than vice-á-versa. Amongst the most common reasons for weak performance on a degree is the lack of movement in regard to study during the early months which leads to a chaotic situation in regard to coursework for the rest of the year. Seek out info on assignment topics as soon as possible (do not wait to be told) and begin your work as soon as possible. Ensure you provide adequate time in your time schedule to undertake assignments that take into account the reading and your analysis and conclusions. Do not write assignments/essays in a day or two as the rushed character of work undertaken in a very short space of time will show and will result in poor marks. Students who rush assignments usually are those who did not begin their work until a few days before the deadline. You must spend ample time reading and preparing your work effectively taking a host of issues, readings and analysis into account.

Ensure you provide ample time to prepare for exams so that your revision is not rushed. If you know what sort of exams you will face you may opt to undertake coursework that is relevant to the exams so that your study and exam preparation are one process that begin from the start of the year though you are of course learning coursework in order to be aware of the subject matter involved which will help you in later studies and work in your profession. You must not take too much time away from addressing areas and issues that you will be assessed and examined in and therefore must strike the right balance between reading vastly in areas that you are very interested in and ensuring you have spent adequate time on the major areas that you will be assessed and examined in.

In regard to time management in respect to reading, 30-40 minutes per session during which time notes are compiled is often adequate and followed by a break of 5-10 minutes during which time contemplation of what has been read and understood and what is to be undertaken in the subsequent reading and you analysis should be undertaken. It is essential to make notes as you read for purposes of learning.

There are invariably times in the day that are most conducive to study. Mornings are superb for studying as you are fresh and full of energy. Afternoons are also of prime usefulness in studies whilst evenings and early night are useful for further work. It may be a good idea to organise particular tasks for particular times including attending to course work and separate sessions each day to build up your overall knowledge and preparation for exams. You must also provide ample time in your schedule for rest between study sessions in the day and evenings and also in relation to the day on the whole. Ensure you are spending time effectively so that you have the time to complete your work to a high standard and also are able to rest. Sleeping only a few hours each night is not helpful for studies nor is this practice healthy.

Try to join at least one university society or club if you are able and to ensure that you have time in your schedule to participate in your society or club. Some societies are very useful for personal development and may aid you in developing skills and coming to learn that much more. Membership of a society often leads to enhanced skills and experience and may also aid you in your future career.

Effective time management at university is not adequate if effective management of your time is not undertaken at home. Hence you must resist the temptation to not bother with studies at home. Your time schedule should include study at home and at university and also en-route to and from university such as reading time on the tube/train/bus. If driving to and from university or indeed to any location you must firmly be fixed on your driving and not under any circumstances be distracted by studies or anything else and must also not engage in phone conversations whilst driving or you may face fatal consequences. The amount of time spent on the tube/train or buses by many people in London or other cities each week amounts to a substantive number of hours which can be used to read a book related to your course or to look over notes (in the case of the latter ensure that these do not fall out during your perusal as once happened to the writer of this work during his first year of under-graduate study). Hence rather than spending much time studying advertisements on the tube/train station or on buses, youwould be well served in going through a general background book for your subject or your notes both of which will aid your overall studies and thought process in relation to your courses. If you opt to read a book en-route to your university or on your way home a light weight book is often handy and practical. In case you are engrossed in your reading on the underground/train or bus (which is a good thing), ensure that you do not miss your station or stop.

Effective time management and effective models of study applied for study sessions will enhance successful performance and reduce difficulty and will serve to help you to avoid panic for the duration of the degree. You must master this element of study skills as soon as possible.

Organise yourself and your time. Become a master of time management.

Manage your time well both at university and at home and in between the two.

Prepare a list of things you must do each week and, if possible, each day. A notebook/PDA (Personal Digital Assistant) made use of for this task and for general notices and information in regard to your studies may be helpful and may well become one of your best friends over time.

Demonstrate and maintain discipline and do not allow yourself to be distracted. Distractions have the potential to lead a person to a failed outcome hence must be avoided. Once your degree is completed you will have much more time to pursue whatever non-study interests you may have.

Justify your use of time. Is any given particular activity useful to your success? Is any particular activity you may be engaged in detrimental to your studies and to you? Think of effect, of consequence and the implications of how you use your time. The results will become apparent.

Demonstrate and maintain initiative.

The above skills must be enhanced during the course of your degree and may be put to good use throughout your careers and lives.

Motivation: Remaining motivated from registration to graduation and job interview

Your studies at university will result in a number of positive outcomes that include:

- A greater level of knowledge and skills.
- You will be acknowledged as a graduate of your subject area.
- The means to begin a career in a particular field.
- The means to further yourself in regard to career.
- The means to undertake postgraduate study.
- A more enhanced world view.
- Greater confidence and means to deal with/address life and the world.
- The foundation provided to you by graduating will aid you for the remainder of your life.

The degree to which you will be able to maximise the above advantages depends upon the precise grades that you achieve as most employers will be seeking candidates for posts who have performed with high and acceptable grades. Hence it is essential that you are motivated and maintain motivation and focus throughout the course of your degree. You must be strong in will and mind to ensure that you leave university with a degree of high standard.

The period of your studies is not a hugely lengthy period of time in comparison to the much longer period of time you have spent at school and will spend at work in subsequent years and decades. Therefore the amount of time you are at university is not indefinite and you must not feel sadness at the period of your university registration and studies in respect to the amount of time your degree studies will take to complete. Think of your rather brief time at university, which will pass very quickly, as a great opportunity and asset in your life that must not be taken for granted nor squandered.

As an educated person you are also able to contribute all the more to your own benefit and that of society and the wider world. These are all further (to the above) good reasons for you to motivate yourself and remain motivated to do well at university from registration to graduation. Do not allow your motivation to waver after the first year as you must remain well motivated to do well in your studies for the duration of your degree. Also ensure that your academic year comprises variety and is interesting. A varied, interesting and stimulating year will also aid you to remain engaged and motivated and will most certainly represent an enjoyable and memorable experience.

Successful research: Gathering & retention of knowledge

Whilst undertaking research may appear an obvious element of study at university, in order to gather knowledge and undertake research robustly to a high and successful standard an effective and comprehensive methodology is required whose key elements may not appear so obvious. The below section provides an insight into how to undertake effective gathering of knowledge and research and how to effectively organise your research and knowledge gathering activity. The aim of this section is to contribute to your insight and ability in ensuring that your time and efforts in research are used successfully for you to build upon during the course of your studies and assessment rather than to be lost a few hours after your research activity has ended through inadequate attention to the recording and absorption of your research. This section of this work will be of use to both the novice researcher and those who already possess some experience of research at university level.

Gathering of knowledge

In order to undertake effective studies it is essential that you are absolutely clear as to what has been asked of you by your tutor/research question or activity. If you are not sure of your work in regard to question or any other element of your task you must speak to your tutor and pay full attention to guidance from your tutor.

The gathering of knowledge represents a most significant element of your studies and reflects the nature of degree level studies whereby it is your responsibility to undertake research for your studies. Your coursework and revision and indeed the bulk of your learning will be very much based upon your ability to gather relevant knowledge (to your question and task) effectively. As you will spend much time each week gathering knowledge you must ensure that your research skills are honed to achieve the most in respect to your research activity in the limited amount of time that you have been provided to undertake your research. You must be clear as to what you have been asked and what course of action you will adopt in addressing the question. Write down what you will do and how you will achieve this and consider your plan carefully in case you are able to improve this plan if you feel it is flawed or inadequate. Do not start your research work (including also for essays) too late or you will not have adequate time to complete your work to good standard and will lose marks.

In order to gather knowledge effectively you must make use of a range of tools available to you that include:

Lectures
Lectures form an important basis for your studies. Attend lectures that comprise a formal part of your course and additional lectures held at your university delivered by guest speakers.

Seminars
The above point also applies in respect to seminars which provide you a means to discuss the subject or issue that each respective addresses.

The library
The library constitutes the most important single source of knowledge for your degree studies and must be visited throughout the week for the duration of the academic year.

The internet
Do not attempt to address your coursework by searching for a website that provides you 'all the answers' as this constitutes plagiarism and could result in your registration at university being cancelled and will also not serve to aid you in the learning process with obvious problems resulting when attempting to undertake further studies or employment. Make use of the internet as a useful source for academic journals, books and information yet also read books and journal articles in print form (where possible) and develop your own work based upon your readings.

Successful study in respect to the above areas is provided elsewhere in this publication.

You may also obtain useful information from relevant documentaries and from purchasing good books from bookshops. It is always a good way to connect to your subject area by building up a collection of books during your studies that may remain a source of reference and interest throughout your life – something I myself have undertaken over the years. Some companies provide first class book purchasing opportunities via the internet.

Magazines and journals
Whilst often not on your reading lists there are usually some very good journals and magazines that are available for purchase at bookshops/major newspaper/periodical outlets. Journals are far more important in academic studies than magazines and are more often to be ordered from publishers or respective institutions and are also usually available in the library and in some cases in electronic form on the internet. There are also some useful academically orientated magazines that are useful for studies for a number of subjects and also serve to keep readers informed of current developments and research in the subject area of the respective magazine. Academic type magazines are available for most subjects across the UK (one of the examples I often cite of the educational richness of the United Kingdom when lecturing at institutions abroad in comprises not only the many fine universities and libraries across the United Kingdom but the sheer number and diversity of good quality publications that are available at good newspaper/periodical outlets across the UK – whose subject matter ranges from the envi-

ronment and natural history to science and architecture) and indeed in many countries. The content of reputable publications in a given subject area is often of the greatest use in expanding your knowledge base, provides you with an additional source of knowledge as well as additional and sometimes very valuable perspective, aids you in framing your own work in regard to conventions and style as well as content of writing, provides your tutors with an indication of your keenness and interest in your subject and very much aids in contributing to your relationship and contact with your subject area. Most academic subject related magazines (such as those that deal with history, architecture, medicine, finance and current affairs) and periodicals offer readers the opportunity to subscribe and in so doing to save a considerable amount of money against the cover price. Some magazines also offer readers the opportunity to join a society which is often beneficial and may add to your background experience and might even make some difference to your future applications for further studies or employment (this is possible though not always so). Magazines do often feature very useful notices and advertisements in reference to conferences, various activities, publications and courses that therefore will aid you in a range of ways in reference to your studies and work and will serve to expand your horizons and perspective. Magazines and periodicals provide a good supplement to your reading but are not to be used in place of your required reading.

The internet also features some (electronic) periodicals which are also a useful source of information and knowledge.

Retention of knowledge

The ability to perform well in your studies rests not only on the ability to conduct research and to attain knowledge but also your ability to retain knowledge. At the core of ability to retain knowledge is the ability to understand knowledge for you will be far easily able to retain that which you understand as opposed to that which you may not understand and may simply seek to remember (by rote without understanding). Whilst I will not go into great detail in the area of connectivity to your subject area on this occasion, due to space, it must be stated that your ability to understand your subject area must draw upon your respect, appreciation and connection to your studies demonstrated by your commitment to succeed in your studies and your ability to apply your studies successfully. Commitment to succeed in studies must be manifest through spending adequate and dedicated time in effective studies (in reference to which this piece of work has been written). Your ability to retain knowledge in reference to your studies must and most certainly will be affected by the manner in which you undertake your studies. Hence if you conduct your studies in an attentive and diligent manner, taking into account at the various points in this publication, you would be more successful in your studies as compared to if you spent very little time on your studies and placed greater emphasis during the course of your degree upon other pursuits that had absolutely nothing at all to do with your studies or indeed if you allocated some time to your studies yet did not devise effective study strategy.

In addition to the various points addressed elsewhere in this publication, successful degree studies will be aided by particular steps that can be taken in order to retain knowledge. Key elements of study skills that aid in retaining knowledge include:

Ensure you make notes as you conduct your reading and studies. These notes should be well organised and structured and most certainly should be written clearly.

The production of a small chart/diagram of how key topics/concepts and issues are related or how a particular issue may be tackled, is most useful.

Try to understand the core basics of a topic or issue before you build up your knowledge in reference to this topic or issue through more detailed readings.

Discussion of your reading and research with peers and with your tutors is most helpful.

Referral throughout the course of the year to your notes and charts/diagrams and further thought and notes.

Further discussion with peers and tutors. What do you know and what is your knowledge of a topic/issue based upon? Apply critical thought and discussion to your knowledge and that upon which your knowledge and understanding is based upon.

Wider reading to understand more about a topic or issue – with notes made following your additional/wider reading.

Constantly think about what you are doing and how your knowledge of a topic or issue is expanding and improving and may expand and improve further.

List what you know about a topic or issue and include the views of key sources for the topic or issue you are dealing with as well as your own views based upon analysis of evidence.

Assessment via peers: Spend some time each week going through your work with a number of (or one) fellow students to assess how much you have learned. Attempt to ascertain what you do not know through discussion of your work with your peer(s) and build up your knowledge and understanding of your identified weak areas so that your mastery of a topic and issue, including in regard to your ability to retain the knowledge of a given topic, is enhanced.

In order to ensure that your continuous acquisition of knowledge of your subject is to a high level and standard you must allocate adequate time in the year to acquiring and retaining knowledge and ensure that your studies are based upon effective strategy including in respect to understanding and retaining knowledge. How you may acquire and retain knowledge is addressed throughout this publication (including in the illustration section).

It should be noted that you will not be able to retain very much knowledge if you allow your studies to be interrupted in the year with numerous activities that are not conducive to your studies and will take you away from your studies. Whilst you will most certainly engage in a range of past times and pursuits (other than studying) during the course of your studies you must ensure that your mind is not distracted from your studies. When you undertake studies for a given study session of around 40 minutes or so ensure that your mind is not distracted by other (non-related) matters which may be addressed after your study session. Focus on the task at hand. Where some time has passed since you have undertaken a study session including reading and note making, spend some time going through your existing notes and readings and also ensure that you are clearly aware of what your next study tasks are. Do not, during the academic year, disengage from your studies for too long a time (not more than a day during term/semester and not more than a few days during holidays during the year). It should also be noted that effective retention of knowledge takes place with careful planning that must also take into account the natural state of your brain. Therefore do not spend more than 40 minutes in reading and note making before taking a break. Before resuming your studies after a break ensure you refresh your mind as to the work you have undertaken prior to your break. Each day of studying should comprise a least 3-4 study or more study sessions of 40 minutes per session. As to what precise activity to engage in for your study sessions various suggestions are put forward throughout this publication which may be applied to your studies in order to aid you in your study strategy and study skills. Consumption of health food and drink during studies is far more conducive to your health than consumption of unhealthy food and drink. Contemplation, during your free time, of how your studies are developing and also of particular issues that your studies are focused towards will also serve to aid you in understanding and retention of knowledge in regard to your studies.

Absorbing and attaining the most from lectures

Lectures (and seminars) form a core part of your degree and provide you a basis for understanding core features of a university course. It is in your best interest to provide priority to attending lectures and seminars and to do so with enthusiasm. Ensure that you are fresh and ready to absorb as much knowledge and insight into the respective area being addressed as is possible during each lecture.

Attend lectures having firstly prepared (reading, writing and thinking) for the questions, topic and issue(s) that will be addressed in the lecture. During the lecture spend more time absorbing and understanding the lecture than preoccupying yourself with attempting to write every word uttered by the lecturer. Write only streamlined notes of the major points of the lecture and expand upon these notes in your own time based upon what you understood of the lecture and further reading. The lecture is delivered to provide you a basis of understanding by way of introduction only and hence must be absorbed fully by listening which is to be followed up by reading. In Britain and in many other countries it should be noted that you are reading for and not listening for a degree. Pay every attention to the lecture and note down the major points which you must then build upon through further reading and understanding through analysis of lectures and reading.

Often, the compiling of a chart – rendering the gist of the lecture into graphical form (see relevant part of illustration section of this publication) – works very well in regard to time management, enabling you to spend more time listening to the lecture and to fully appreciate later on, what you have recorded onto paper of the respective lecture.

Handouts

Tutors often provide handouts in relation to topics that are covered in respective lectures or seminars. Whilst not a book that features a glossy cover, a handout from a tutor is a valuable tool in unravelling and unpacking a specific topic or issue and therefore must be treated with care as something of value. Handouts must not be treated as the sole source of information on the subject they deal and must be supplemented with additional reading. Handouts therefore serve as valuable guides and a useful introduction to a topic or issue and should be built upon with further reading, discussion and thought. In order to attain the most from a handout you should read through and underline key terms and information which will serve as a useful pointer when you return to the same handout at a later time. Underlining key terms and information also serves as a useful way to understand and absorb the contents of the handout. They must therefore be studied thoroughly based upon a sound methodology of reading, absorbing, writing comments on and understanding. Handouts provided by tutors should also be used as a guide to producing your own handout when you may be asked to do so during the course of your degree (if this is the case for instance in relation to a presentation you may be asked to provide in a seminar). Ensure that you do not lose handouts as they will be very useful for your studies and exam preparation. Placing all handouts into a box file or similar storage unit will help you to ensure you do not lose handouts. Using particular box files or other types of storage to store handouts and other information for a particular course will also help you in regard to organisation of your studies. Each box file or storage unit should be clearly labelled to avoid confusion.

In regard to compiling a handout, see below, under *presentation skills*.

Effective note making

Further to the above, ensure that your note making is highly organised with a system developed to provide you with a clear understanding of a lecture/seminar and your reading. Hence you must work out what the introduction and defining points of a topic are and what the major questions and issues are. Perhaps underline this element or use a particular coloured pen. Clearly state what the major elements to the topic are and who some of the main names/writers are as well as the title of book and year of publication.

Learn to be concise in note making so that you do not spend endless time writing too many words. Write down the major elements and points and spend more time listening to your tutor and working out what is being addressed. Note down some key observations you may develop about the topic and link to previous reading you will have undertaken with key words in relation to information or an author of a book. Draw lines depicting branches of a topic (see 'spider diagram' in illustration section of this work) rather than attempting to write lengthy sentences when you make notes which will take too much time up. Try the above a few times and enhance your own system of note making so that you understand as much as possible of the topic and so that these notes make perfect sense to you in 6 months time even if your fashion habits in respect to your attire have changed and you are using different coloured pens. Use pens for note making that you are comfortable with and that do a good job such as a set of coloured ballpoints.

Enhancing communication: Written and oral

Always begin your written work with a clear plan in mind. A draft of a plan is a good idea and allows you to consider and adjust your plan before starting your work. The more you read and discuss as well as constantly think about a topic or problem the more you will be able to understand your work and the easier it will be to conceptualise and render your work into writing. Whilst time is required to understand a subject you should always try to begin your assignments as soon as possible and continue your work until you reach a satisfactory set of conclusions, based upon analysis of evidence. Your assignments must also feature your own opinion and judgement in view of the evidence. Be analytical and not descriptive and above all, be original.

Your writing at university level must demonstrate use of good English grammar and punctuation, clear understanding of the subject area you are writing on, evidence that you have read the required reading and understood this (make use of both journals and books) as well as evidence of analysis and satisfactory conclusions.

You must be methodical in your writing demonstrating a step-by-step approach and understanding to the question that is being asked. Always ensure you understand the question and that you answer what you have been asked. Writing at degree level must also comprise clear and also concise sentences and paragraphs that are not too short or too lengthy. You must also develop your writing so as to be able to compose elaborate sentences – yet ensure that elaborate and substantive writing is clearly understood.

Before you begin your work you would be advised to outline the problem, your argument and organisation of work in the form of a short abstract of a short paragraph in duration, in italics, and entitled, 'Abstract'. Whilst you must also demonstrate stamina in your writing and an interest in the work via your style and content, word length must always be adhered to so that you can demonstrate your effectiveness in writing in timed and controlled conditions. You must manage your written work with effective time management and ensure that you write a good piece of work that makes clear that you understand and answer the question and therefore is wholly relevant to the question, possesses depth, evidence, analysis, conclusions yet undertaken within a reasonable amount of time. In other words you cannot spend a year to write a good essay. Hence a good answer plan and schedule must be prepared that you adhere to and sits well with the other course work you are undertaking. Also ensure you develop your academic writing and avoid informal and journalistic writing style.

Read through your work and make any adjustments before submission of your work and try to arrange an informal group of peers who can read your work and offer their comments and to do the same for their work. Input as the result of discussion with fellow students (your peers) can be helpful particularly at the start of a course and also helps to build up contacts. Ensure that your work is not repetitive and is comprised of well-argued points based upon evidence and your own analysis and conclusions.

Do not waste time during even the early weeks and months at university in non-university-related pursuits so that you end up with a mountain of course work to do half way into the term or semester. On the contrary, ascertain from an early stage in the course what work you must do, even if you have to ask your tutors before you are told, work out your entire coursework requirement for the year for all courses and how much time you will allocate each week to what. Also inquire as soon as possible in regard to what the exams will cover and ensure your study of the course and exam preparation are one and the same process. This way you will save time and be on top of both your coursework and exam preparation. You are most certainly interested to study the course in order to attain knowledge and insight into your area of study yet must also take into account you will be examined and assessed and therefore must ensure that you prepare adequately in your studies for assessment and examination.

Make sure you keep to the word limit as set by your course tutor. Always undertake a word check of your work and rigorous editing before you submit your work or you will lose marks.

Writing a scientific paper

A scientific paper should be clear, simple yet comprehensive, well organised and systematic. A scientific paper should provide information that allows the reader to assess observations, carry out an identical experiment and evaluate the intellectual content and structure. The paper should possess an introduction, material and methods as well as results and discussion (known as IMRAD). The title should possess relatively few words. The paper should begin with an abstract that summarises the contents of the paper whilst the introduction provides background on the topic being dealt with, the rationale for the paper and also the scope of the work and its aims and hypothesis. The introduction should also provide an outline of how the reader is to evaluate the results of the study. The materials and methods section of the paper should provide adequate and clear information about what was undertaken and how this may be repeated. The results in the paper should outline the work undertaken and date that derives from the work. The discussion provides a description of the results and also identifies relationships between data and comparisons with other data as well as clear and concise conclusions. Any lack of correlations and exceptions should be stated here. The conclusion should summarise the results of the paper. Ensure that the paper is supported with references both within the corpus of the paper and also in the bibliography. Illustrations and tables are also essential in scientific papers.

Referencing

One of the major differences between academic writing and general writing (including many pieces of journalistic writing in newspapers) is the presence of formal academic referencing throughout any piece of academic writing. Referencing provides the reader (your tutor) the means through which to ascertain the sources of information for your work and demonstrates you have read and are applying the knowledge from your readings before conducting your own analysis and critical evaluation of your sources. Your tutor must be aware from your writing that you have not only read the important sources for the subject of your writing but also what in your writing comprises the words of your sources and what particular part of your written work is your own work. It is therefore essential that your work is referenced throughout. The presence of references also protects you from accusations of plagiarism (copying the work of others and contending that the work of others is your own work).

Referencing your essays and dissertations must be undertaken in a formal academic manner. There are a number of methods for referencing your work. The basic rule in respect to academic writing and referencing is that you make clear citation of the origins of any text or point made in your written work that is from a book or journal (or any other form of periodical/publication or the internet). The name of the author, date of publication, name of publication, place of publishing and name of publisher and page number comprise the core information for an effective academic reference. A reference may take the form of a footnote placed directly after the text which derives from or is a word-for-word citation of the words from a book or journal (or internet site). In this case the reference ought to comprise (see below example of an academic reference in the form of a footnote): The Harvard system is widely used in many universities in the present time and comprises reference within the body of your text rather than below your text in the footnote. An example of the Harvard system of referencing for the same text that is used in the footnote reference: The historical problem is simply that science does not stand still (Crump, 2001:127). A space between the colon and page number may also be applied (Crump,

2001: 127). In the Harvard system of referencing less information is included (surname of author, year of publication and page number) as compared to the information that a full reference featured in the footnote comprises. However the core information that your tutor requires is contained in the Harvard system of referencing whilst the full information of the text or journal cited is featured later on, in the bibliography of your written work (see below). At the present time the Harvard system of reference is deemed to be satisfactory by most universities. It is advisable to check with your university department as to what form of referencing they prefer their students to use in their written work. You may also attain view academic books and journals and consider how these works are referenced. It must be noted that a good piece of academic writing should comprise at least 4-5 references (if not more) per page. See below under bibliography, in reference to use of *et al.* as substitute for listing a book edited by several authors (when citing such a book in your reference).

Bibliography

All your written work that is submitted for formal assessment (assignments, dissertation) must be accompanied by a bibliography. The bibliography represents the means by which you display the books and journals that you have read for your work. Bibliographies must ideally include the most important publications that are relevant to your piece of work and also any other related materials. You must ensure that core readings on your reading lists are included in the bibliography. You must only include in your bibliography those books and journals that you have actually read and cited from in your work. A typical assignment should comprise a bibliography of at least several if not 10 books and a few journal articles (2-4) if possible. A dissertation should include a bibliography of at least 30 books and several journal articles, if not more.

The bibliography must be produced in a formal academic manner. Consultation of academic books and journals will provide you an insight into academic style for bibliography.

A typical academic bibliography for a book comprises the following information and style:

Crump, T. (2001) *Science: A Brief History*. London: Constable and Robinson Ltd.

The name of the text should appear in italics.

A typical academic bibliography for a journal comprises the following information:

Wrangham, R.W., *et al.*, 'The Raw and the Stolen, Cooking and the Ecology of Human Origins', *Current Anthropology*, vol. 40, 1999, pp.567-594.

The name of the journal and not the name of the article should appear in italics or be underlined.

The use of *et al.* designates there are more than one author. All authors may be listed in the bibliography for this text yet *et al.* may be used to substitute the entire list. If *et al.* is used the first author of the list of authors for a respective book or journal must feature followed by *et al.* The same may be said for use of the Harvard referencing system in respect to referencing. Rather than listing several authors of a book (if edited by more than author you may state the name of the first author, followed by *et al.*).

Oral skills

Good oral skills involve clear and measured speech that is not too rushed nor too sluggish, is concise yet also elaborate when you are illustrating a point, though always relevant to the topic.

Verbal communication in academia is more formal than everyday casual conversation (as formal academic writing differs from informal writing) yet must possess a pitch and character that is conducive and of interest to those who will be listening to your oral presentation. It is important to have a good idea of what you will say and to base your verbal delivery upon some form of plan - written or within your mind. Reading and preparing your work before speaking is always a good idea as is making notes as to how you feel your oral delivery went and how you feel you may improve. Never be shy to ask what people thought of your work (friends tend to always smile and say 'fantastic' whilst others in the group may be more frank).

In order to attain experience of how your oral delivery is performed you may wish to record yourself speaking on an academic subject, play back and make some notes on the strong and weak points both of which must be strengthened. Indeed a good place to begin to improve your oral presentation is to undergo this process so that you may be able to devise an action plan to improve. It is also advisable to share the recording with your peers in order to attain feedback as, in similar respect to appraising your own writing before submission, you may not manage to identify all the weaknesses in your work and what you fail to spot the first time may also pass you by on subsequent occasions (the advice of a former tutor that I readily apply to my own work to the present day). When considering your own voice in order to ensure that your effort to improve your speaking is enhanced, consider the following issues:

Volume

Are you speaking too loud or not loud enough. In an oral presentation you will probably not have your voice enhanced by a PA or microphone/speaker unless you are delivering a formal lecture. However you must ensure that you are speaking loud enough so that what you are saying is not lost upon the audience due to their inability to hear you. On the other hand you must speak too loud as this would be inappropriate, may be considered by your audience to be impolite and after a short time you may not be able to continue to speak very loud. Pause and allow, through your silence, for the audience to absorb your points as you move along.

Pace

You must not speak too fast. One of the key areas to master in study skills which will serve you well in both studies and future work and life is that of time management. In regard to oral presentation you will have much to say yet restricted time to do so. Hence you have to plan well what you need to say and what should not be said. You must ensure you have adequate time to cover the essential issues and therefore must be concise and thought provoking. Be conceptual and concise and do not provide a lengthy narrative that will be of little relevance and usefulness.

Quality

It is essential that the content of your presentation is of the highest standards and quality as you will be judged and marked against this key element. The quality of well researched work is sometimes lost due to a poor quality of oral presentation. For guidance in regard to presentation aids see the relevant section of this work. Quality of oral delivery is also essential. Hence your voice must be audibly clear. Do not speak to loud or harshly. Speak clearly and smoothly. Vary your voice when you deal with key terms or concepts so that you place emphasis upon the significance of these terms or concepts through the additional volume you apply. Speaking at the same volume or same pitch for the duration of your oral presentation is ill-advised as this will result in the loss of impact of your presentation. Hence learn to vary the pitch of your voice in relation to the structure and content of your presentation offering a varied repertoire of volume and tempo throughout which will enhance your oral delivery very much, providing of course that you have researched well and have organised your presentation well enough.

Those who attend your oral delivery will need time to absorb your points. Hence it is essential that in order for others to adequately absorb your oral delivery you provide some pause between your sentences and points in order to allow, very literally, for pause for thought. Do not bombard your audience with too much information and no pause for thought. Indeed too much information bereft of structure and context and information that is not relevant nor explained well enough will not aid your presentation. Hence be very thoughtful and critical of what you will say and how you will convey what you will say.

Control

You must demonstrate that you are in control of your oral presentation by being versant in your subject area (attained by diligent and robust study and practice of your presentation) and following a clear and effective plan of presentation (which you may etch out on paper in the fashion of a lecture plan with specific time allocated to respective elements of your presentation). Exercising control also requires paying attention to the audience (good eye contact demonstrates that the presence of your audience matters and will result in a better rapport and interest from your audience) and ensuring that the audience are paying attention to you/how the audience is responding to your presentation. Do not be afraid to ask any person who is rude enough to start a private conversation with another participant to pay attention to you. This may be done in the first instance by a look in the direction of this person followed by a request that all pay attention.

Further points to consider in regard to oral presentation

♦ Body language is also an essential element in your oral presentation. Be attentive and focused towards your audience. Stand robustly and do not appear sluggish in regard to your stance and overall posture. Do not place your hands in your pockets. Face the audience and if possible, move across the area you are speaking from. Make use of your hands in expressing yourself yet not excessively so.

♦ Ensure you are well presented in regard to your attire.

• Effective oral presentation takes time to attain mastery in yet will improve over time, as with other study and presentation skills, providing you plan and execute your methodology and organisation of your oral delivery effectively.

• Practice in writing, reading and oral delivery helps to develop these important skills. You may also make notes of your observations of how a number of lecturers speak and present both at university and also in other arenas such as on television (in reference to academic/academic based presentation) and identify some key pointers.

• It will be useful to make use of visual aid in your presentation – the benefits of and guidance for which are outlined elsewhere in this work.

• If you are asked a question the answer to which you do not know, do not shy away from your lack of knowledge but do try to offer a suggestion as to where the student or member of staff may go to ascertain the answer to their question such as a particular writer/book. You may sincerely state that you have thus far not researched the particular issue that has been asked of. Your sincerity will be appreciated. Do not attempt to bluff your way through as this may result in the overall impact of your presentation being lost. World authorities in various branches of knowledge do not know everything of their subject area – neither will you.

Effective analysis

Analysis is the examination of the elements or structure of a phenomenon, subject or issue (or substance or property) in respect to university studies. Effective analysis results in a greater understanding of what you are studying. Effective analysis careful consideration and critical thought and appraisal of the subject matter that is analysed and involves asking and addressing a range of questions in respect to the topic or issue you are dealing with. You must be able to break down and understand the inter-relationship between the constituent parts of a phenomenon, subject or issue (or structure or property) in order to be able to effectively analyse in respect to your studies. One of the aims of your degree studies is to ensure you have mastery of your subject area and are competent to ask the right questions of a subject or issue as well as to be aware of the answers to these questions.

When you enter into analysis approach a subject or issue with an open mind and tackle from a variety of aspects. Single track analysis seldom generates impressive results. Consider the subject or issue from a holistic perspective taking various issues and elements into account. Think about what you are seeking to achieve in your analysis vis-à-vis the aims of the work you are engaged in. Are you seeking to prove or disprove? Are you seeking to assess, explore or investigate? How reliable are your sources of evidence? What are your aims and what is your methodology?

19 Enhancing Study Skills

KEY STUDY SKILLS

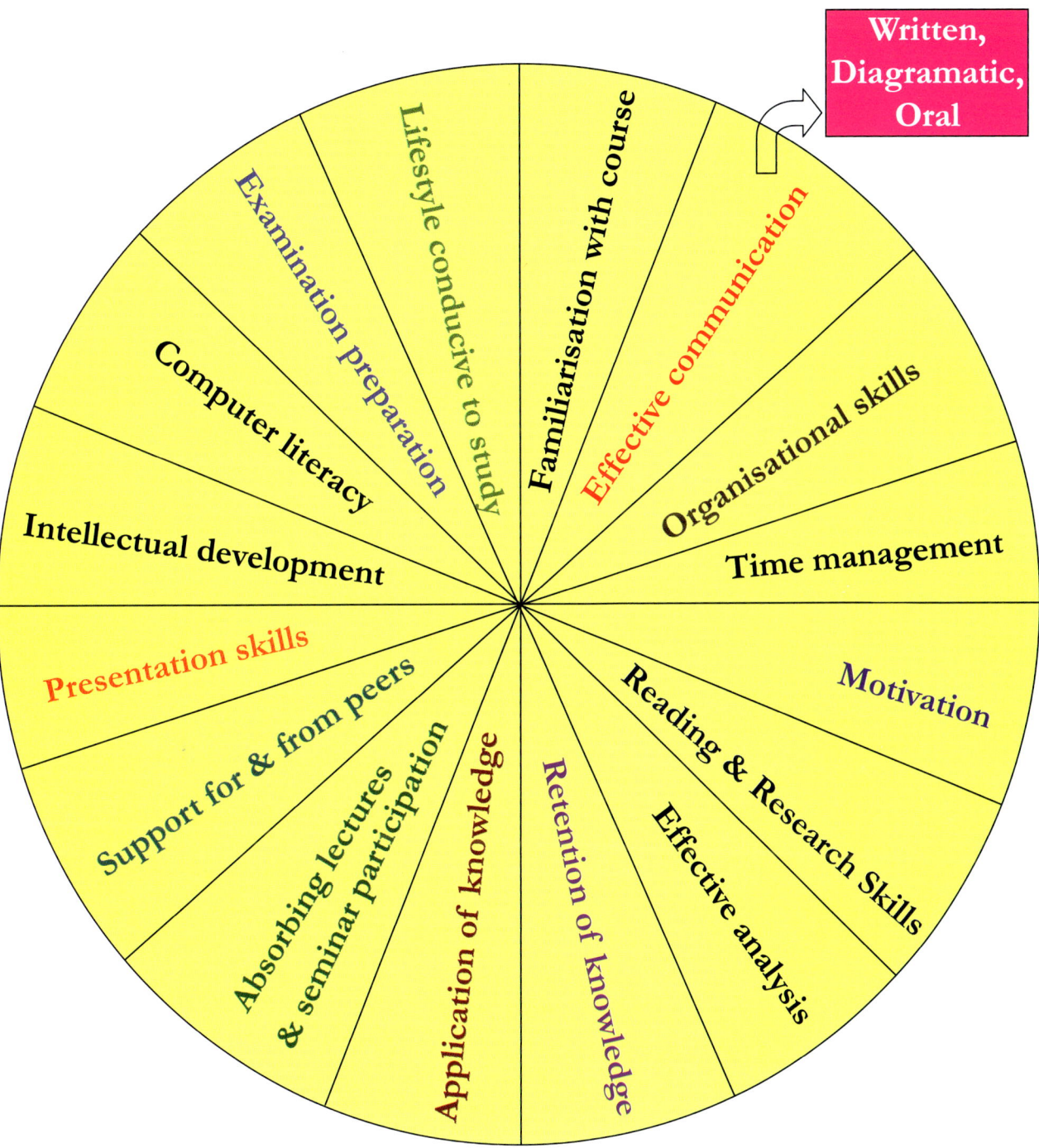

Written, Diagramatic, Oral

Also: Taking the initiative, Guidance from tutors, Note making, Effort, Dedication, Commitment, Determination to succeed.

Concentration, Creative thinking & writing, Critical thought

© Farhat A. Hussain 2007

21 Enhancing Study Skills

Be relevant
Be critical
Be systematic
Remain within word limit

*Present analysis in academic manner.
*In regard to your writing be clear, concise and provide evidence of your argument.
*Make use of data and references.
*Make use of charts, graphs where applicable.

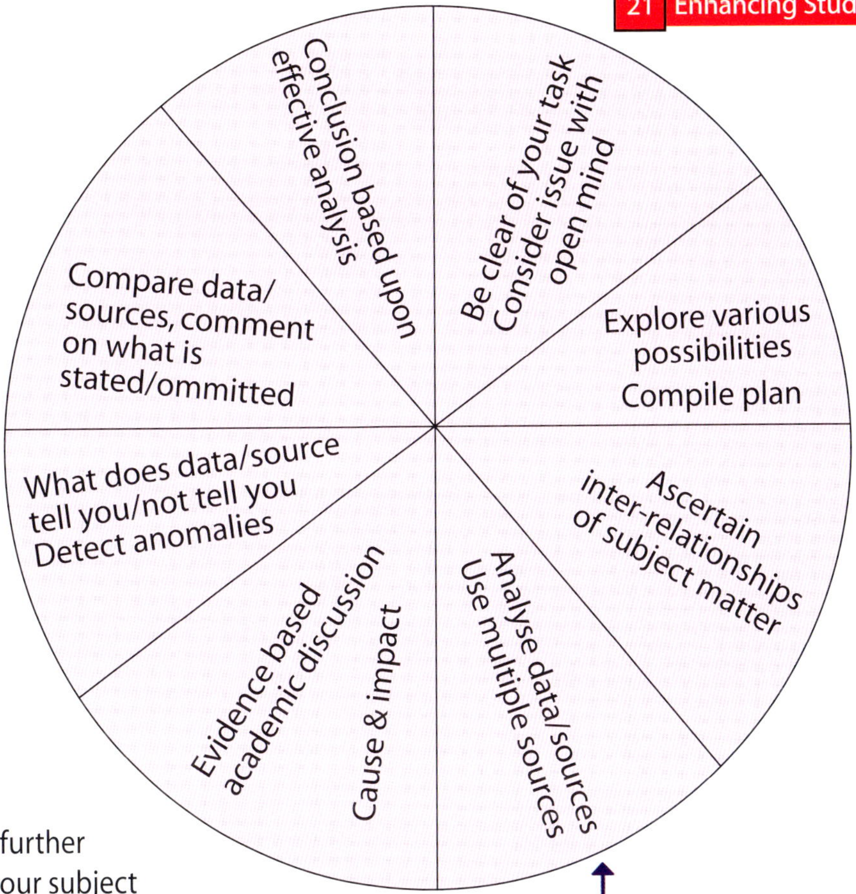

Consult academic journals for further insight into academic analysis in your subject

Effective Analysis wheel:
- Be clear of your task / Consider issue with open mind
- Explore various possibilities / Compile plan
- Ascertain inter-relationships of subject matter
- Analyse data/sources / Use multiple sources
- Cause & impact
- Evidence based academic discussion
- What does data/source tell you/not tell you / Detect anomalies
- Compare data/sources, comment on what is stated/ommitted
- Conclusion based upon effective analysis

EFFECTIVE ANALYSIS

Allocate adequate time to write

Effective Writing wheel:
- Understand aims
- Read well (many sources)
- Make notes and think about issues
- Design a plan
- Be well structured
- Effective use of grammar
- Be coherent
- Be consistent
- Be systematic
- Be clear
- Be methodical
- Be definitive
- Be relevant to question
- Include references
- Include bibliography
- Read through before submission

*Elaborate sentencing where helpful.
*Varied sentencing stucture.
*Effective use of grammar.
*Accurate punctuation and spelling.
*Argue well with rationale and evidence.
*Engage in academic discussion & analysis.
*Be concise.
*Elaborate your point with evidence & academic discourse.

Adhere to wordlength   Do not plagiarise   Illustrate work where appropriate

EFFECTIVE WRITING

© Farhat A. Hussain 2007

LECTURES

Lectures constitute a major element of your studies at university. You must be aware of the format, organisation and role of lectures. You must ensure that you attain the most from all lectures.

Come prepared - read up on subject of lecture from more than one source. Arrive on time. Concentrate. Ensure you have paper and a pen. Whilst writing on file paper is fine, it is also useful to write your notes in a dedicated notebook so as to reduce the possibility of losing pages and in order to ensure that your work is readily available under a single cover. Make notes (essential issues and subject matter). Ensure you are listening for guidance from your lecturer on topic of lecture. Focus your mind. Do not waste your time attempting to write down every word spoken by your lecturer as the aim of the lecture is for you to listen and absorb. Write down the most important points, issues and questions (questions made known by the lecturer of a topic or issue and/or your own questions that emerge from the lecture).

Listen to your lecturer and understand. Ask any questions you may have from the lecture or from the related reading you have undertaken. Follow up each lecture with discussion with peers, your tutor/lecturer where practical, further reading. Ensure your lecture notes are kept in a safe place. Make use of your lecture notes in your coursework and exam preparation. Whilst lectures are important for your studies you must also ensure that you are engaged in a substantive amount of reading each week.

Lectures serve to provide a basic foundation of topics within your subject area whilst reading provides you with greater insight into particular issues and branches of topics.

It is of the greatest importance that you demonstrate the utmost courtesy to your lecturer, fellow students and subject matter. Arrive on time for your lecture and do not chatter/talk during the lecture. Attend all lectures.

SEMINARS

Seminars provide a unique opportunity for you to interact with your tutor, other students and the subject of your studies within an academic setting. Seminars represent one of the most significant parts of your week at university and will contribute very much to your learning at university.

Attendance at seminars (and lectures) is of great importance for your studies and must be undertaken with the greatest diligence and interest. Absence from seminars (and lectures) will result in your falling behind your course and may result in penalties by your university towards you including a weak reference if you fail to attend. Come prepared to seminars. Ensure you know what topic and issues are to be covered. Conduct preparatory reading and make notes. Also note down any questions of a topic or issue that arise from your preparation.

Out of courtesy for your tutor and other students and in order to ensure your successful participation, you must arrive at seminars on time.

In your seminars, make notes of the core issues and subject matter. Raise questions if you have any. Do not shy from speaking, sharing thoughts and questions. Also allow other students to speak and show courtesy through listening and respecting the views of others. Write down useful comments from fellow students. Ensure you actively participate in your seminars by reading up in advance and making your points and thoughts known via your oral presentation. Use of *PowerPoint* presentation may aid your presentation as will provision of a handout for your tutor and fellow students. Follow up each seminar with further reading, discussion with peers and tutor (in person or via email). Ensure you are aware where your seminar notes are as you will need to refer to these notes for coursework and examination preparation. Peruse through your seminar and lecture notes every so often for recap and further consideration of the subject matter.

WRITING AN ESSAY

Do not start your essay too late

MAIN THRUST OF YOUR WORK

Before you begin ensure you make a plan of your essay, also read extensively

SECTION OF ESSAY	MAIN THRUST OF YOUR WORK
Title	Ensure you are clear of what you are being asked. Ensure your answer is structured to answering the question.
Introduction	Define the question. Identify key debates and issues. State what you will do. Define key terms.
Corpus/main body of essay	Engage in academic discussion of the subject of your essay. You must articulate the main points and arguments of your work in this part of the essay. Provide evidence and ensure you analyse the evidence in your discusson. Be relevant, critical, concise and analytical.
Conclusion	Summary of main points. Consider the major issue and what your essay has identified in view of the question. Highlight any anomolies/issues raised. What does the essay demonstrate in reference to the question asked?
Presentation	Ensure your work is presented in the prescribed academic manner as outlined in your course handbook. Ensure your work is well referenced, the bibliography is adequate and that you have edited your work before submission. Submit a draft if possible for comment and improvement.

© Farhat A. Hussain 2007

25 Enhancing Study Skills

- *Be relevant
- *Be critical
- *Be audible
- *Use diagrams/illustrations

- *Be polite.
- *Listen to others when a suggestion is offered.
- *Absorb feedback and improve.
- *Do not seek to glorify yourself but to address the aim of the academic discussion/issue.

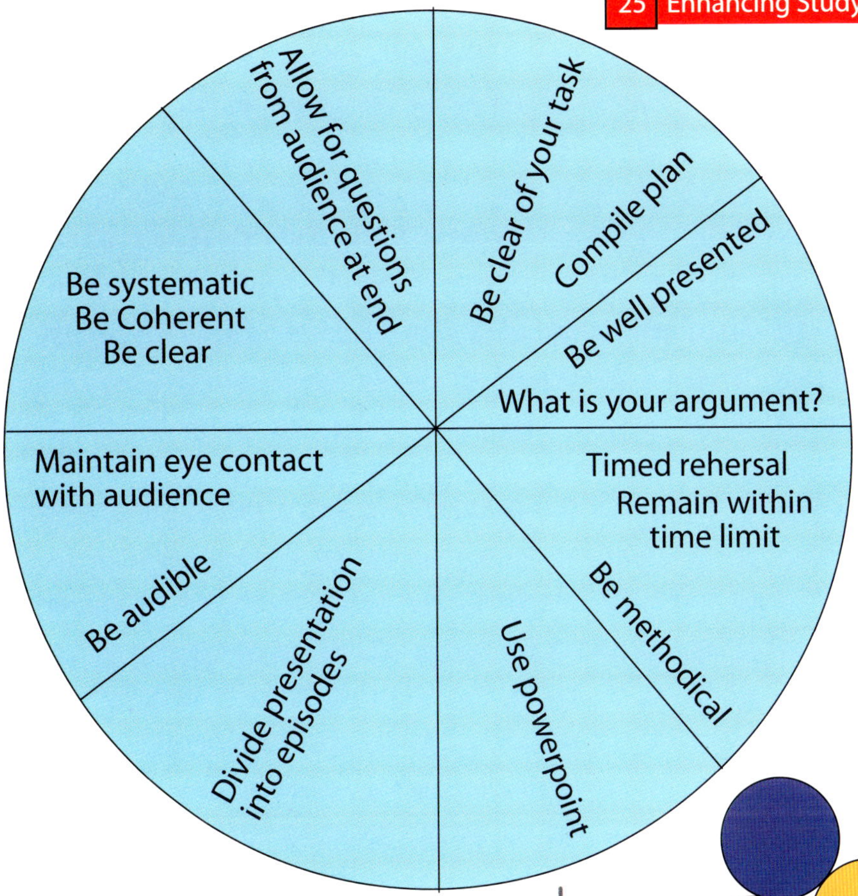

Effective Oral Presentation wheel:
- Be clear of your task
- Compile plan
- Be well presented
- What is your argument?
- Timed rehearsal — Remain within time limit
- Be methodical
- Use powerpoint
- Divide presentation into episodes
- Be audible
- Maintain eye contact with audience
- Be systematic, Be Coherent, Be clear
- Allow for questions from audience at end

Attend academic lectures and seminars in order also to attain greater insight into oral presentation - be perceptive.

EFFECTIVE ORAL PRESENTATION

POWERPOINT Presentation

Engage your audience

Engage your intellect
Engage your creativity
Maintain eye contact
Maintain your smile

Keep within time limit

Be Concise. Be audible.
Avoid using too many words.
Use your text as pointers from which you may elaborate in your oral presentation.
Use light text on dark background.
Divide presentation into episodes.
Ensure each slide is well defined & well arranged.
Use illustrations.
Constantly face the audience as you are speaking.

© Farhat A. Hussain 2007

REMAIN MOTIVATED:

From your university degree interview to your job interview and beyond...

Believe in your ability to contribute to your subject area and your chosen profession.

*Your degree will not last forever - do not waste or lose a day.
*Your degree will help you in future life, studies and work.
*Your degree is one of the most important investments you will make in your lifetime.
*Knowledge, skills and experiences attained & developed during the course of your degree will aid you significantly in the future.
*Vary your time on your degree so as to ensure each week is a new and welcome challenge.
*Meet the challenge of your degree and succeed.

Greater effort,
greater concentration
& effective studying
= Greater understanding
of your subject, better grades
and comment from
tutors and better results
and references from your university.

27 Enhancing Study Skills

If you are experiencing difficulty in your studies: Some suggestions

Be constantly mindful of time and what you must achieve each week. Maintain focus and work hard.

- **Do not allow problem to persist without attempting to remedy before you have lost far too much time.**

- **Identify the problem. Be searching and accurate in your assessment.**

- **If straight forward matter of insufficient time for deadlines you must place more emphasis upon studies.**

- **Be realistic about your studies and place greater emphasis on addressing your studies during course of degree - cut down on non-essential areas that will hamper your studies.**

  Prioritise & implement.

- Success in studies = Success in life

- **Consult fellow students for their suggestions in regard to your problem. Speaking to others is good.**

- *Master your studies, achieve, succeed & prosper.* **Consult with your tutor. Accept advice of tutor and work hard to implement.**

- **Identify your problem. Ascertain how to deal with problem. Deal with problem. Learn from the experience.**

  Be content & happy.

Specific areas of issue/concern may be addressed in respective parts of this study skills publication or by consulting with your tutor.

© Farhat A. Hussain 2007

Concentration

SUCCESSFUL STUDY REQUIRES CONCENTRATION
(in respect to focus and attention of your mind to a particular task)

Achieving & enhancing concentration
Ensure you are in a quiet place.
Switch your mobile phone off.
Ensure you are comfortable.
Ensure your brain and body have received rest and food/drink before you being your task.
Focus the mind to your task:

Identify your task
-Consider what is involved.
-What is the best approach?
-What must you do?
-How much time is needed?

Spend some time to think about your task
-Write down your thoughts
-Focus upon your thoughts vis-á-vis your task.
-How may you improve your thoughts further?
-Be relevant.
-Be critical.
-Continue to hone your thoughts as to your task.

Block out distractions
-Other activities and thought may be undertaken later on.

© Farhat A. Hussain 2007

How to develop concentration

Focus upon a single object
-e.g. the patterned shape on this page.
-Think about this shape, size, colours, shade
and anything else that comes to
mind about this object.
-Do not allow your mind to be distracted.
-Do not be distracted by the colour of the
background to this page or other objects.
-Maintain your focus upon the patterned shape.
-Write about this shape (not about it's
surrounding colours and objects).
-What thoughts come to mind
in reference to applying
this patterned shape to anything in your life,
work and/or interests?
-Think and then write.
-What defines this patterned shape
vis-á-vis it's surroundings?
-How is this patterned shape different or
similar from it's surroundings on this page?

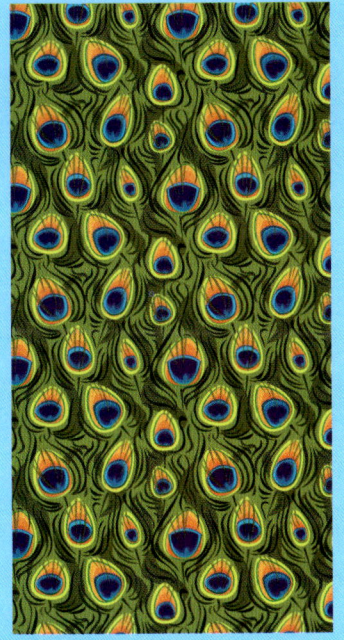

How to sustain concentration

Continue to focus upon your specific task.
-Block out all irrelevant thoughts and distractions
(if it is too noisy move to a quieter place).
-Discipline yourself to give full attention
and full effort to your task.
-What are you doing?
-What must you do now and where will it lead to?
-What is your aim?
-You must continue your work but
may require a short break before you resume.
-During your break do not engage in other
mental activity of substantive level in another task.
-During your break continue to reflect and to focus on
what you have undertaken so far.
-What are your conclusions thus far?
-Continue with your task until you
are satisfied with the results
(you may require another break).

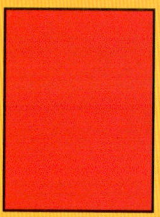
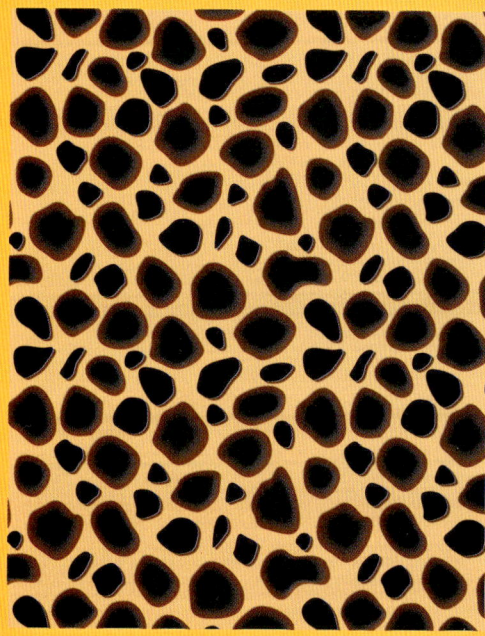

How to **enhance** concentration over **extended** periods
(further to the above)

The greater practice you have in concentrating upon tasks the more enhanced your ability will be to concentrate effectively and to concentrate for longer periods of time.

- Focus and master your mind.
- You must strengthen your mind and faculties through mental exercises and challenges of a varied and sustained nature.
- Begin with easy tasks such as the above and then move onto more complex tasks. e.g. What does the array of objects on this page illustrate to you? What may you add to this array of objects that may enhance this display - why so?
- Be critical (how similar are the objects on this page with previous pages? why so/why not?)
- Be searching, be diligent, be focused, be articulate (in your thoughts and in your notes and written and oral presentation - including in your levels of concentration when engaged in these tasks.
- Concentration must be applied in all your academic activity).
- Be mentally awake and alive (ensure your mind receives adequate mental exercise through a range of mental tasks that are stimulating and challenging). Your mind is your major asset and will enable you to succeed in your studies and in life.
- You **can** and you **will** concentrate and succeed.

© Farhat A. Hussain 2007

31 Enhancing Study Skills

You are a student at universtiy.

You have personal and family responsibilities & interests which must also be addressed.

You must address the range of responsibilities that you have, participate in your areas of interest, develop as a balanced and rounded person with a range of interests and skills.

You must also succeed in your studies through constant effort, discipline, management, organisation, thought and focus.

Remain focused

- Be critical
- Devise effective plan
- Identify your task
- Awareness of time
- Do not be distracted
- Maintain focus
- Give time & effort
- Be intellectually rigorous
- Succeed in your task
- Implement plan
- Take break then onto next task

© Farhat A. Hussain 2007

PEER SUPPORT

Providing and participating/benefiting from peer support represents an essential element of degree studies.

Whilst you are primarily responsible for your own studies it is useful for you and for your fellow students (peers) to support one another during the duration of your degree through a number of ways that include:

DISCUSSION, READING OF WORK FOR BOTH ABSORBING ADDITIONAL PERSPECTIVE AND KNOWLEDGE AND IN ORDER TO OFFER YOUR SUGGESTIONS TO YOUR PEERS OF THEIR WORK IN REFERENCE TO CONTENT, STRUCTURE, GRAMMAR AND PUNCTUATION.

The more involved you become in the work of your peers in the above context the more mastery you will attain of your subject area. Whilst spending time conversing with friends of social issues etc is always a welcome break from studies your discussion with fellow students on your course of key aspects of the course will aid you and your fellow students very well.

PEER SUPPORT IS USEFUL BOTH IN RELATION TO THE COURSES YOU UNDERTAKE DURING TERM TIME, DURING BREAKS BETWEEN TERMS AND IN REFERENCE TO BOTH COURSEWORK AND EXAMS.

In respect to peers, aiding one another in studies will contribute to your successful understanding of a subject and will also serve to strengthen bonds with other students.

© Farhat A. Hussain 2007

PEER SUPPORT

Peer support may be provided in person,
over the telephone, via email.
Peer support may take place in a variety of locations
throughout the day, week and term-including on a train and bus
on your way to or from university, during a break from lectures or
seminars, in the library (do not disturb others!).

Practical considerations must be taken into
account in reference to peer support.
Separation of peers by distance may be
overcome by telephone whilst very lengthy peer
support via telephone may result in a substantive phone bill.
A combination of face to face discussion, use of email
and phone provides for a relatively comprehensive system
of peer support in regard to access. However ultimately the level of
success and assistance provided by peer support depends upon
the organisation and effective use of time with peers.
Peer support must focus upon your academic work.
You must prepare a clear agenda and collectively work through this agenda
during peer support. In regard to tackling a major piece of reading
for example, each person (whether there are two, three or more persons)
may read a specific section of the reading before commenting to the
group - though a second opinion is also useful.
Be as critical as possible based upon evidence
and seek to reach definitive conclusions. Due to the usefulness of peer
support you ought to place at least one session of studying or discussing
studies with fellow students per week into your weekly planner.

Peer support is to be made use of in conjunction with attendance at lectures,
seminars, supervision from tutors for the course, your personal studies.

For the duration of your studies you must build a
successful relationship that involves the subject area
you are studying, your peers, your tutor and yourself.
Employers are always keen to accept those who are able
to perform well as individuals and as part of a team. Peer
support is therefore of great use during and after your studies.

DURING THE COURSE OF YOUR DEGREE IT IS YOUR RESPONSIBILITY TO UNDERTAKE YOUR COURSEWORK AND EXAMS SUCCESSFULLY. PEER SUPPORT IS USEFUL YET MUST NOT BE CONFUSED WITH YOUR OWN RESPONSIBILITIES IN REGARD TO YOUR DEGREE.

BOOKS

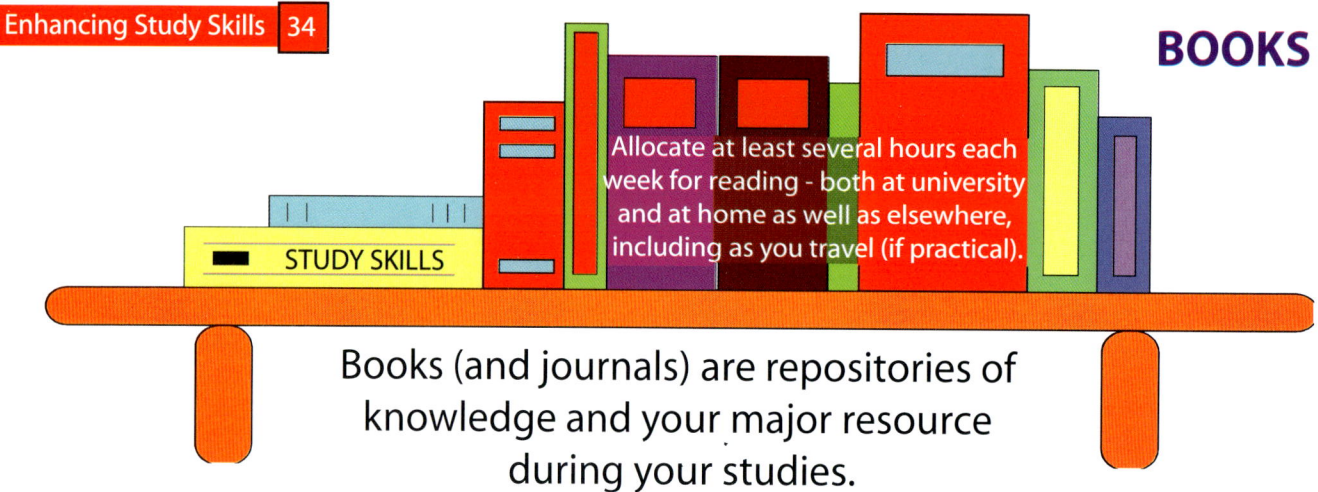

Allocate at least several hours each week for reading - both at university and at home as well as elsewhere, including as you travel (if practical).

Books (and journals) are repositories of knowledge and your major resource during your studies.

At British (and indeed at many other) universities students are reading and not listening for degrees. Whilst lectures and seminars are of greatest value and form an essential aspect of study at university, reading books and journals and critically evaluating as you read constitutes the core of your learning at university as you build up your knowledge base. Your coursework and examination performance is based upon what you have read and your ability to absorb, understand, criticise, synthesise and apply this knowledge.

Know which books you need - consult your reading list, find them in the library, buy them, read them (relevant parts first), value them, learn from them, evaluate and appraise them. Keep the books you buy and treasure them for the rest of your life. Buy a bookcase.

You must allocate adequate time each day for reading in order to attain a good grasp of your subject area -including the various issues and debates that concern respective branches of your degree. Consider carefully also how academic writing is undertaken as you absorb the contents of books and journals you read. Make notes of what you read.

Whilst reading from a number of books and journals is helpful in building up your knowledge base you must attain an understanding of core issues for a given topic or area before you delve into the range of views expressed in various books and journal articles. Whilst reading books and journals is a pleasure you must not allow yourself to be distracted from your task by stumbling across interesting yet wholly unrelated material at a time when you must undertake an assignment or prepare for a seminar or an examination.

Marking Criteria

It is essential that you are well aware of the criteria for marks for your coursework. You must strive to attain the best marks. An awareness of the marking structure will aid you in the preparation of your coursework.

The below mark structure is typical for an Arts and Social Sciences based degree course in the United Kingdom. A similar marking scheme is applicable for examinations. Some universities operate a more particular marking scheme than that outlined below. It is therefore essential to obtain a formal marking scheme from your department.

Class of mark (Also grade & mark band)	Criteria
A/70%+ First Class	This work demonstrates a very high competence in the major issues that the question sets outs. This work demonstrates a thorough understanding of the topic and presents a very clear, thought out and concise argument with ample evidence of thorough reading and understanding of reading. Original analysis of material is evident with a good insight into theoretical concepts and the ability to apply them in the analysis of evidence. Well presented and effective use of referencing. Illustrations present to a high standard where applicable.
B/60-69% Upper Second Class	This work demonstrates a good grasp of the subject with clear evidence of reading of relevant materials and critical evaluation of reading material. Some presence of independent thought and application in appropriate sections of work. Presence of analysis of evidence/data. Well presented and well referenced. Some arguments could be better articulated and dealt with more thoroughly.
C/50-59% Lower Second Class	Demonstrates a good grasp of main issues yet does not appear to be very well read. Some effective use of reading and application to the issues yet not substantiated. Conclusion is relatively weak. Structure is also lacking and very basic as is bibliography and references. Some evidence of critical thought and use of evidence/data.
D/40-49% Third Class	Use of some evidence/data in addressing the question. Structure is lacking and arguments not developed. Conclusion insubstantial and lacking in adequate evidence. Demonstrates some acquaintance with literature yet also evidence of insufficient reading and application of evidence/data. Poor presentation with numerous mistakes in grammar, spelling, punctuation. Incomplete bibliography. Little evidence of critical thought.
E/below 40% Fail	Very weakly written with no evidence of understanding of major issues nor reading of main materials. Poor structure and poor conclusions. No evidence of critical thought, poorly referenced. Inconsistent and incoherent. Marred by many typographical errors. Poorly presented.

© Farhat A. Hussain 2007

Getting the most out of feedback

University tutors will provide you written feedback on marked work that conforms to university regulations. Feedback is provided in a manner that reflects the strengths and weaknesses of your work so that you may improve your work. You must not merely look for your mark on a marked piece of work but must also read through the paper to assess comments provided by the tutor throughout your work and also consider carefully the formal statement of feedback your tutor has provided. Absorbing feedback from your tutor and improving your knowledge and future performance is an integral and essential aspect to study at university level and represents a major study skill. Self reflection and self improvement are essential study skills and will facilitate improvement (one must think of the learning curve).

Read through all your feedback and comments on all pages of your marked coursework. Think carefully about the comments your tutor has made.	Ensure you are quite clear as to the feedback and comments of your tutor. If in doubt, or disagreement speak with your tutor.
Pay attention to all feedback and comments. Consider if there is any feedback that is surprising to you.	What are the areas of weakness in your work your tutor has identified? What areas of strength in your work have been identified?
What are the most serious issues of comment of your weakness identified by your tutor in your coursework? Pick out and focus upon two or three main comments.	Formulate action plan to strengthen your existing strengths and to address your weak areas in regard to presentation, punctuation, grammar, structure, content, methodology, relevance, argument, analysis and conclusions in your work.

In subsequent coursework you undertake be mindful of previous feedback from your tutor/s and your propsed action plan to improve your work. Ensure you provide adequate time to undertake your coursework.

© Farhat A. Hussain 2007

37 Enhancing Study Skills

INTELLECTUAL DEVELOPMENT

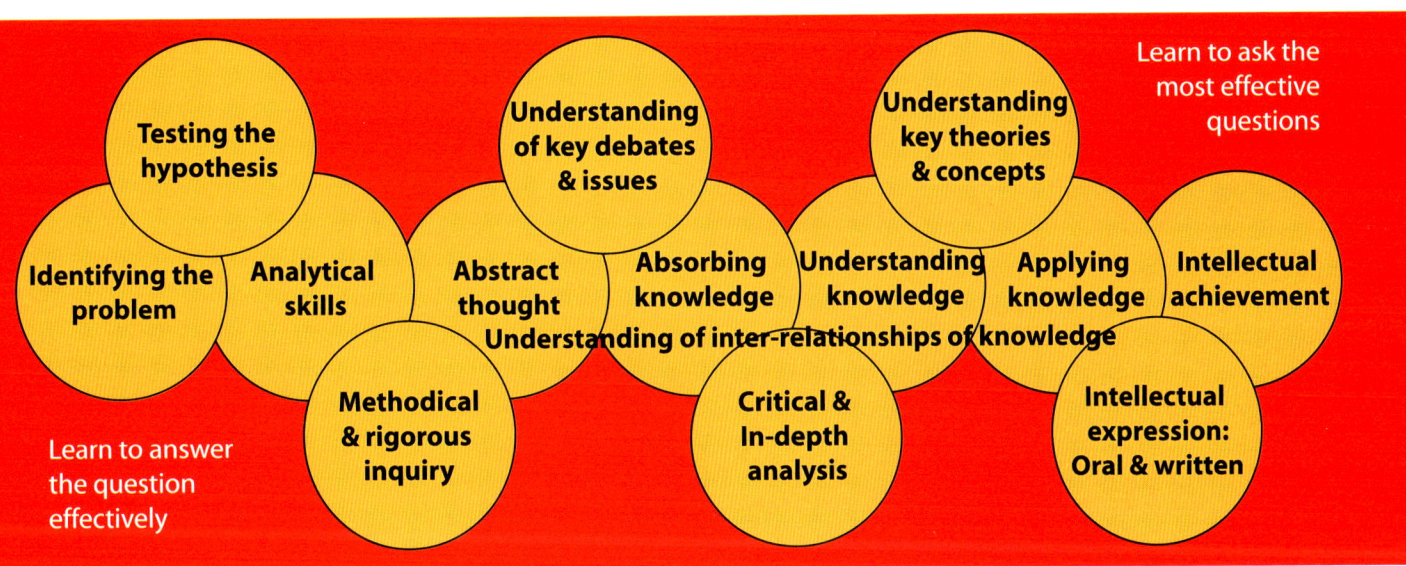

Development of intellect throughout course of degree

Commencement of degree → End of degree

Organisational skills

Identify your needs
Plan your course of action
Make notes
Allocate adequate time
Work to deadlines
Apply your plan of action
Maintain focus
Assess your performance
Enhance your performance

© Farhat A. Hussain 2007

SELF-REFLECTION

In order to progress in your academic work you must consider your performance throughout the year. You must also consider how you may improve your performance.

How are you progressing? How do you know this? -Grades, comments from your tutor.

Are you on schedule? If you are behind, why so? If you are on schedule what else can you do?

SELF REFLECTION

How do you feel? Are you content with your studies? If not, identify the issue (s).

Produce an effective action plan to address areas of weakness and to strengthen your studies.

Reflect upon your work and progress on a daily, weekly, monthly, termly and annual basis.
Consider your strengths and weaknesses, build upon the former and address the latter.
Study well and also live a happy and holistic life.

© Farhat A. Hussain 2007

Numeracy

 The ability to be numerate, irrespective of your respective subject area at university, is an essential skill and trait that is of the greatest use in studies and life.

 Even if your degree does not comprise any direct application of numbers you ought to ensure that you are able to perform basic arithmetic tasks to a good standard as part of your overall education skills.

Respect for others

At university you will come across tutors and students who are from a wide variety of backgrounds including different countries, religions and cultures. You will also come across people who hold different views to your own in respect to your subject areas and much else.

It is essential in respect to your character building and in order to attain the most from your university education that you provide respect to all your fellow students and university staff. The wide variety of people you will come across will serve to enrich you and will prepare you well for the wider world once you complete your university studies. It should also be pointed out that most employers relish employing those who are able to respect and get on with those of various cultures and backgrounds. Respect for others is therefore a virtue and should be adopted. Positive interaction with those of different backgrounds, in particular different cultures, is enriching and of mutual and lasting benefit to all concerned.

Note making via diagrams

In order to be concise and conceptual in your note making so that you are able to arrange your notes in an organised and effective manner particular types of diagramatic representation may be used (see also concept mapping).
Examples of a spider and tree diagram appear below and overleaf respectively.

Spider diagram

Example: Notes on subject of rise of clinical medicine

The branches or legs of the spider diagram demonstrate some core issues/books that pertain to the subject matter of the spider diagram

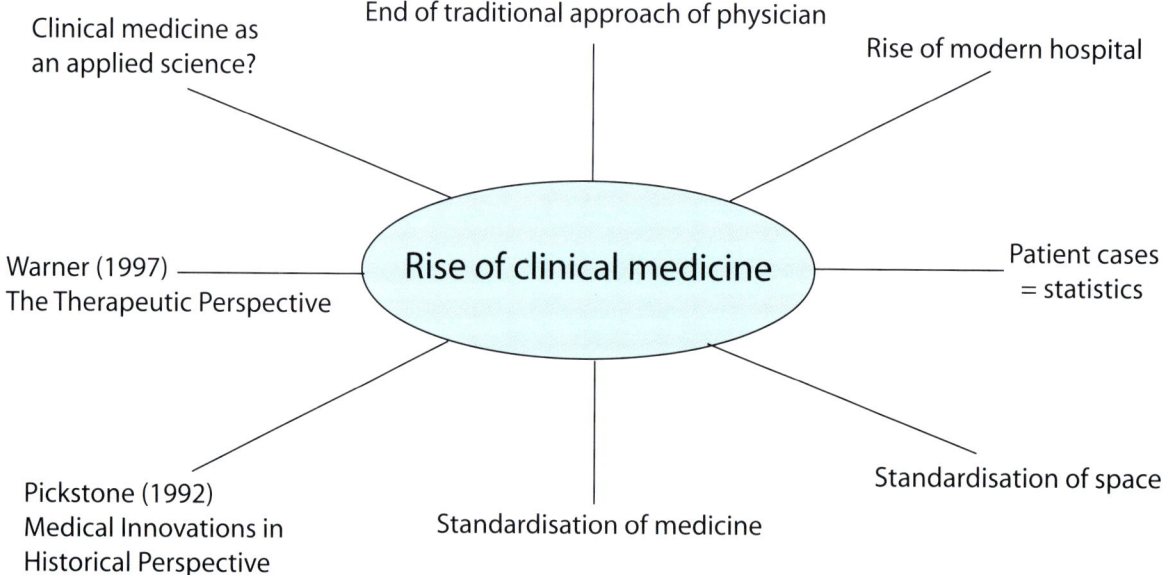

This form of diagram is easy to articulate and to absorb when viewed at a later date. Spider diagrams are therefore very useful tools for note making and understanding as well as revising key issues or topics.

© Farhat A. Hussain 2007

Tree diagram

Example: Notes on subject of rise of clinical medicine in Western Europe in the 19th century.

The branches of the tree diagram demonstrate some core issues/books that pertain to the subject matter of the tree diagram. Each branch at the top of the tree diagram branches off to form a further set of topics/issues of the respective sub topic.

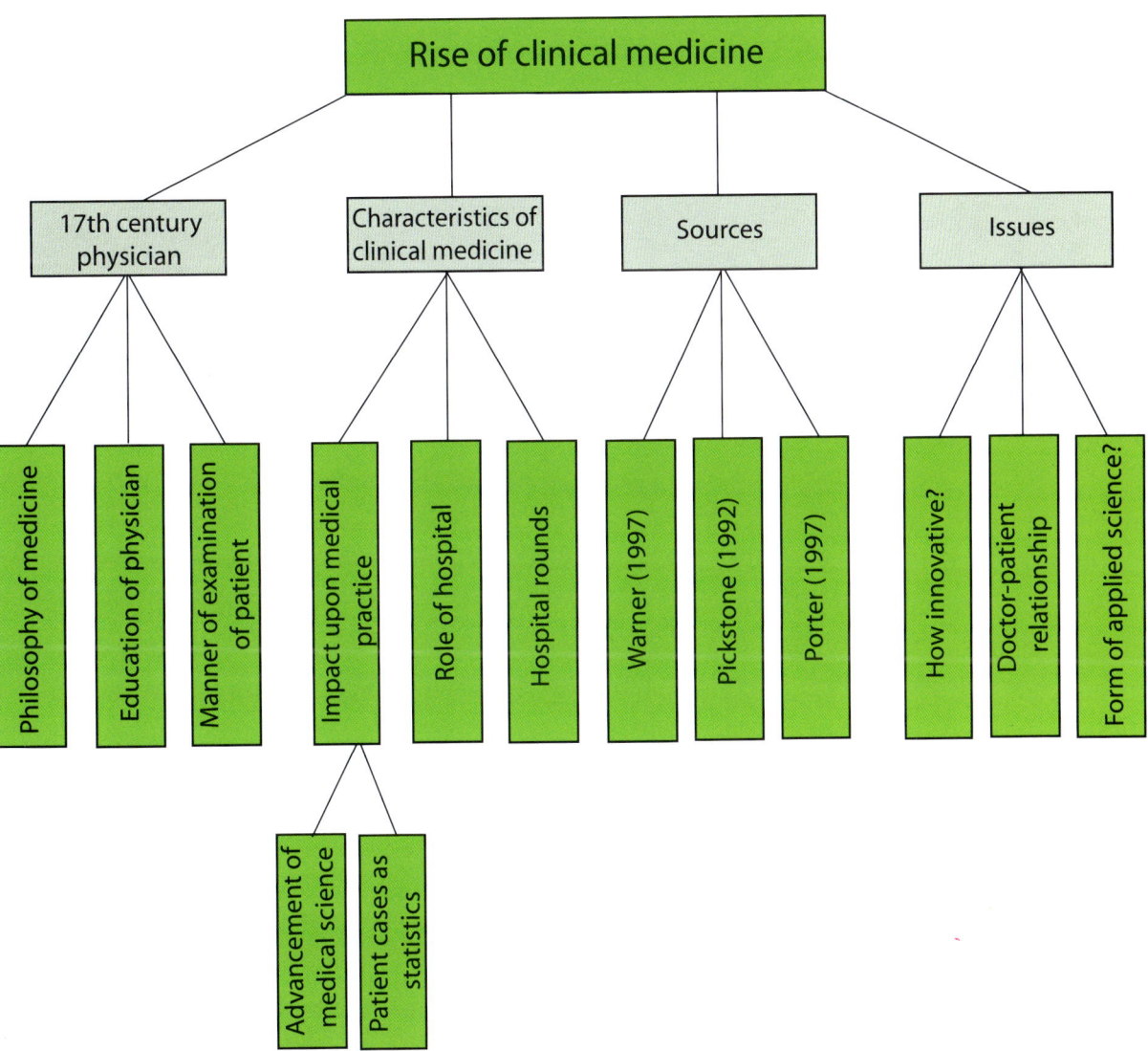

Tree diagrams may comprise a variety of numbers of layers of branches (three major layers in this example with fourth layer present in reference to 'impact upon medical practice').

This form of diagram is easy to articulate and to absorb when viewed at a later date. Tree diagrams are a little more sophisticated and comprehensive than spider diagrams (the latter of which comprises a set of branches that stem from a single topic). Tree diagrams are helpful for providing students the means to group related issues vis-a-vis particular headings and sub-topics. Tree diagrams are therefore most useful in providing substantive organisation of a topic or issue, both for initial understanding and for revision.

© Farhat A. Hussain 2007

Concept Mapping

A useful way to understand a body of information is via a concept map. A concept map renders the essential elements of a subject or issue into key headings. Each heading designates a branch of the respective subject area or issue. The concept map provides a handy overview of what a subject or issue comprises including the inter-relationships of the various areas that the respective concept map comprises. Consider the subject or issue carefully as you plot your concept map. Add to the concept map as you attain more knowledge. The aim of the concept map is to understand what the subject or issue comprises and the inter-relationships/dynamics of the various parts of the respective subject or issue. A concept map is also useful for testing hypothesis and for planning.

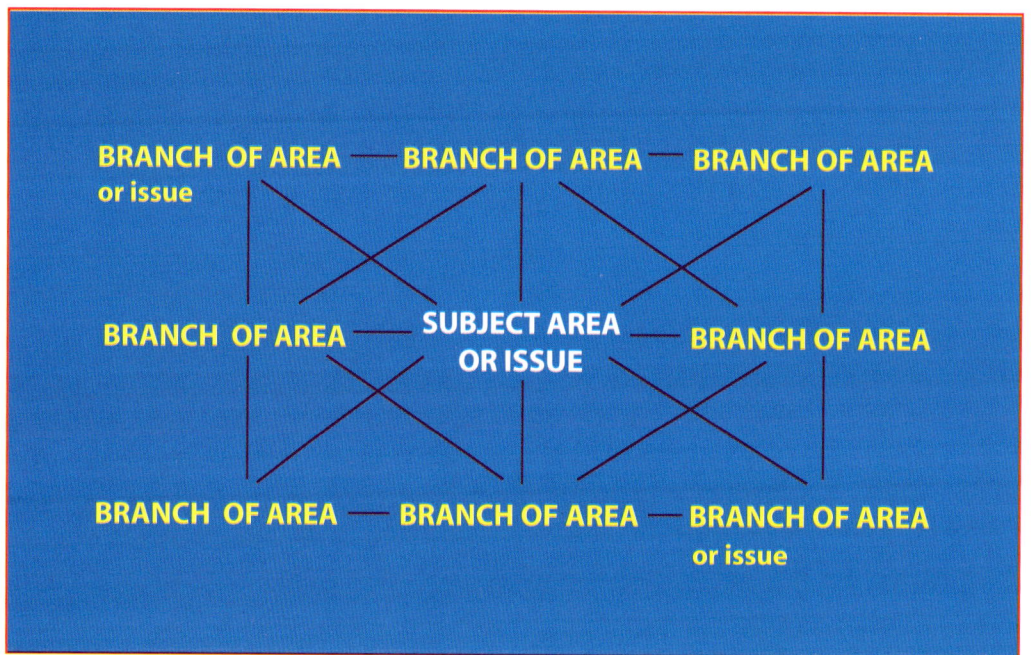

Example of concept map (from history of medicine study by author of this work):
Information:
The ancient Greeks are thought to have advanced medicine in a number of key branches that include medical theory, diagnosis of various disease, conception of the body, medical ethics and medical technology. Yet very little information survives from ancient Greece in regard to hospitals. Whilst some of the medical work undertaken by the ancient Greeks was based upon rational science, the ancient Greeks also made reference to superstition. Moreover it is considered that elements of medicine in ancient Greece were influenced by medicine in the ancient Middle East, in particular from Mesopotamia and Egypt.

It must be noted that the concept map on the opposite page represents a brief example of what may result from the above outline of information. Key issues include organisation and understanding of knowledge.

Concept map for the above information appears on opposite page

© Farhat A. Hussain 2007

Concept Mapping

Medicine in ancient Greece

Key Themes:
- Medicine and society
- Medicine and the state
- Medicine and religion
- Superstition

Impact of diet

Disease - Conception and diagnosis of, cure for, spread of. Evidence from skeletal remains

Zoonotic disease: What the sources say

Public and private hygiene and sanitation

Gender and health

Key strands:
- Theory
- Practice
- Ethics
- Technology
- Education

Formal training
Private education

Surgical instruments
evidence v interpretation

Key medical authorities: Hippocrates

Medicine and war
role of surgeon
field hospitals

Doctor-Patient relations
Compensation to patient if doctor performs mistake
Enforcement by state

Areas not addressed by Greeks

What the primary sources say:
Herodatus on advanced medicine in Egypt

Advances undertaken by Greeks

Existing medical knowledge, practice and technology:
Egypt - influence upon Greece
Mesopotamia - influence upon Greece
Phoenicia

What the secondary sources say:
Professor J. Sournia
History and archaeology of medicine work of Farhat A. Hussain
Professor other opinion

Other points and possibilities to consider
Pharmacy
Dental care

Impact of Greek medicine upon Romans
Interaction of Greek and Indian medicine

Origins of the hospital as institution for medical care

© Farhat A. Hussain 2007

Enhancing Study Skills 44

THE UNIVERSITY LIBRARY *Silence at all times*

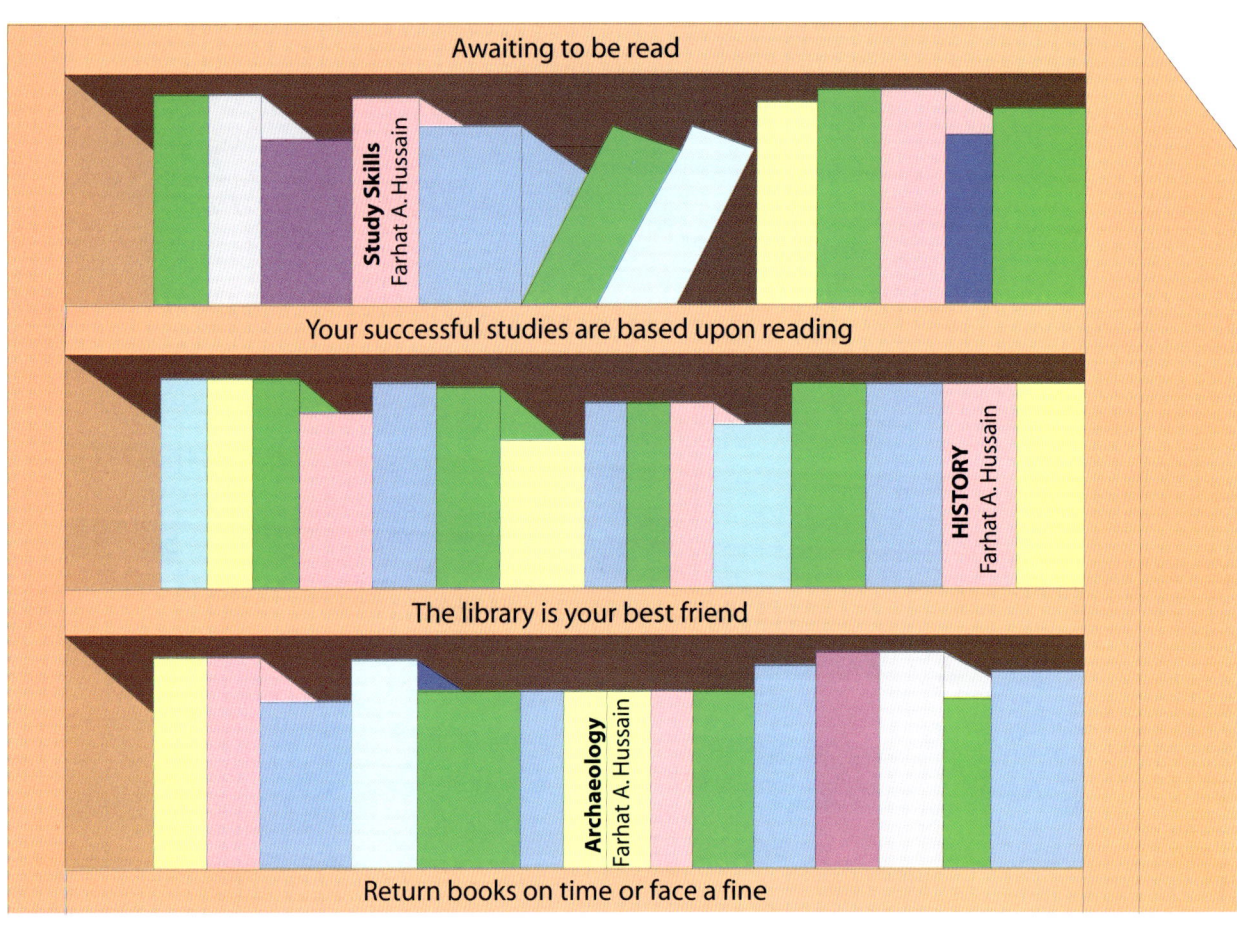

Awaiting to be read

Study Skills — Farhat A. Hussain

Your successful studies are based upon reading

HISTORY — Farhat A. Hussain

The library is your best friend

Archaeology — Farhat A. Hussain

Return books on time or face a fine

Come prepared with a study plan.

Maintain discipline – be true to your studies and to yourself.

Select a pen you are comfortable with making notes with.

Use of a laptop for your work is helpful yet may be noisy and therefore a distraction for others in library.

Think about your academic tasks – what do you wish to do.

Read widely and be critical of your reading.

Build up your knowledge base and your academic ability.

THE UNIVERSITY LIBRARY

The university library is the epicentre of your studies

At the start of your degree ensure you are familiar with the layout of the university or university college library.

Ensure you are aware of where all relevant book and journal sections for the subject of your studies are located.

Do not shy away from asking library staff of location of books.

Obtain a plan of the library/library guide which will also provide useful insight into the organisation and procedures of the library.

The library is also a useful place to engage in your studies.

Find a quiet place to study - think carefully of your aims.

Be respectful to other students - do not make too much noise.

Spend a good 40 minutes studying before taking a short break and continuing your studies.

Visit the library at least a few times each week.

Treat your books with the utmost respect.

Make notes, think about your readings, discuss with peers.

Return books you may take on loan on time and undamaged.

Membership of specialist libraries may also prove helpful.

Literature review

Undertaken in order to demonstrate your knowledge of the topic of your research. Also undertaken to demonstrate your ability in respect to analysis and interpretation and also synthesis and critical appraisal.

Key features of literature review

Reading for your literature review

Good literature reviews are based upon appraisal of a number of leading pieces of literature on the subject of your chosen topic.

Ensure you select a good range of books/journal articles but do not attempt to take on too much to read. Justify your choice of literature for review.

Record the bibliographic details of your literature thoroughly.

Organising your literature review

Synthesise themes from your reading. Cluster these themes via:

List of topics.

Concept map
(see relevant section of this work).

Be clear as to what your aims are and organise your review accordingly.

Structuring your literature review

Begin with a general review of the literature you are dealing with.

Move to a more specific study of the literature.

Ensure you are critical and conceptual.

Organise your paragraphs along thematic lines.

Your review must take the reader step by step through the literature.

Features of a good literature review

Relevance to topic you are dealing with.

Concise treatment of the work you are reviewing.

Clarity of expression, use of good English.

Critical of the work of the writers.

Well referenced review.

Evidence of your independent analysis of subject.

Literature reviews may take the form of a book or article review.
(see also respective part of this work that addresses book review)

BOOK/JOURNAL ARTICLE REVIEW

In many university courses students are required to carry out book/journal article reviews as a formal exercise (in reference to university study of all subjects critical study of books/journal articles also constitutes a form of book review). A formal book/journal article review undertaken for a university course is geared towards achieving a number of objectives for students. Book/journal article reviews assess the ability of a student to conduct critical reading of a particular book or journal article and to provide a report of the book or journal article that has been read in the form of a review. The review must be well structured and well written in a cohesive, systematic and easy to follow style and must enable the reader to ascertain the aims, key elements, analysis and conclusions of the book or journal article.

However a review is more than just a summary and must critically consider the book or journal article. What are the aims of the work? What are the strengths and weaknesses of the piece of work? How clear are the arguments? How sound is the evidence, analysis, methodology and conclusion? To what extent have the aims of the book or article been addressed? Reviews must be conducted in an academic manner and must adhere to a specified word length. Hence another aspect of a review is to be able to understand and make critical study of a piece of work in a specified word length. Your review of a piece of work must be well written so as to engage the reader. Once you have written your review ensure you edit and review your review until you are satisfied with the standard and effectiveness of your work.

Provide your review to another person for review! The ability to undertake effective reviews represents a major study and academic skill and should ultimately inform your own writing and knowledge. Whilst reviews do not constitute the major part of your assessed work you must not underestimate their value nor the amount of time you will require to undertake a review.

Enhancing Writing: Elaboration

Elaborate writing is an essential writing skill that will greatly enhance academic performance. Writing must comprise a balance of short and elaborate sentences. Short sentences demonstrate you are able to be concise whilst elaborate sentences demonstrate your intellectual ability to communicate your point comprehensively. You must be aware of when to write a short sentence and when to write an elaborate sentence. An effectively written paragraph will comprise sentences of varied length. Elaborate sentences also provide readers more information and greater discussion of the subject matter being addressed.

	Subject matter: Empire of Alexander of Macedonia (early 4th century BCE)
Underdeveloped	Alexander ruled.
Basic	Alexander was ruler of an empire.
Developed	Alexander of Macedonia ruler over a vast empire.
Elaborate	In the early fourth century BCE, to his death in 323 BCE, Alexander of Macedonia ruled over a vast empire that stretched from Greece to India and encompassed a vast number of lands and people.
Highly elaborate	By 323 BCE, shortly before his death, Alexander of Macedonia had conquered a vast area that encompassed Macedonia, Greece, Egypt, Syria, Mesopotamia, Persia, Central Asia and Afghanistan which all became part of his vast Empire and ultimately benefited from the fusion of Hellenistic and Middle Eastern culture and civilizations with lasting impact for many centuries in a number of key areas.

The underdeveloped sentence is far too short and provides little information on the subject matter. The basic sentence provides concise information on the subject matter yet very little by way of elaboration. The developed sentence provides more information than the basic sentence and whilst still quite a short sentence does feature a more elaborate character than the basic sentence. The elaborate sentence provides the reader with more information on the subject than the previous sentences and is elaborate in its character and prose as compared to the previous sentences yet is less elaborate in character, prose and length as compared to the highly elaborate sentence which provides far more information and retains balance in respect to grammar and structure of the sentence. However this sentence is also relatively long and may be split into two sentences. An effective elaborate sentence must convey information, discussion and argument clearly, cohesively and effectively and comprise effective grammar, prose, structure and word length.

Effective writing comprises sentences of varied length. Even elaborate sentences should not be too lengthy. Ensure that your sentence articulates your point or points effectively and clearly. Ensure you provide evidence to support your points. Ensure your work is well structured. Be relevant and critical. An elaborate paragraph comprises a comprehensive and substantive addressing of a particular issue but must not comprise a single sentence but rather an effective combination of elaborate and short sentences.

© Farhat A. Hussain 2007

Enhancing Writing: Varied Grammar

Elaborate writing is an essential writing skill that will greatly enhance academic performance. Writing must comprise varied grammar so as to demonstrate your mastery of the English language and your ability to communicate effectively. Constant repetition of the same grammar throughout your work must be avoided. Vary the choice of words that you use so as to provide your marker with evidence that you are able to communicate your thoughts with competence and mastery of the English language. The development of varied grammar is also helpful in respect to oral communication. Indeed the building of your ability to acquire and apply varied grammar for writing and in speaking often come hand in hand. Inhibition in speaking elaborate English in respect to grammar must be considered before you deal with improving your ability to speak and write elaborate and varied grammar. Educational research demonstrates that there is a connection between choice of grammar used in writing and speech patterns.

Sources of influence of choice of grammar upon your speech	Early learning and schooling, reading (formal/academic and non-academic literature), television/cinema, oral communication with friends and peers drawing upon some of the above.

You must distinguish between informal oral communication with friends and peers and also that which is used on television (in respect to informal language used) and formal academic writing.

	Subject matter: Empire of Alexander of Macedonia (late 4th century BCE)
Underdeveloped	My feeling is that Alexander ruled.
Developed	Based upon the evidence it is clear that Alexander of Macedonia ruler over a vast empire during the fourth century BCE.
Elaborate	It is quite clear from the evidence that, in the early fourth century BC, Alexander of Macedonia ruled over a vast empire that stretched from Greece to India and encompassed a vast number of lands and people.

The underdeveloped sentence comprises a very small variety of words that are also unqualified in respect to evidence. This sentence lacks developed grammar as compared to the developed sentence whose choice of grammar is varied and measured. The elaborate sentence comprises a good range of grammar that serves to provide clarity and elaboration of the points that are being made in regard to the subject matter and issue that this sentence seeks to address. The developed and elaborate sentences constitute formal academic writing in regard to their composition and style whilst the underdeveloped sentence comprises words used in informal conversation. The elaborate sentence also comprises effective punctuation (also important).

Effective grammar may be developed via practice in respect to formal academic writing which itself may be developed through reading good quantities of academic writing in academic books and journals (and also reading of formal newspapers and magazines) and greater participation in academic discussion and writing where emphasis is placed both upon content and composition as well as style. Activities geared towards enhancing grammar, such as reading and commenting upon written work via academic discussion, should be undertaken in conjunction with fellow students. Use of slang and informal English in your academic work must be avoided (both in respect to academic discussion and academic writing).

© Farhat A. Hussain 2007

Enhancing Study Skills 50

Examination Preparation for end of year examinations

Enjoy a well deserved break

Examinations — Be clear, comprehensive yet concise, be orderly, use evidence, analysis, firm conclusions, be calm!

Maintain focus
Maintain concentration
Maintain understanding

Go through all your work in an orderly and scholarly manner. Ensure your work flows through your mind.

Ask your tutor for time to discuss your exam preparation. Clarify what you have covered and seek advice as to any potential areas of weakness.

Maximise time spent on exam preparation. Cut down on many other activities by this time.

Go through course and exam prep notes. Ensure you have mastery of major debates and issues and you are able to write comprehensively with authority with clear analysis and sound conclusions based upon analysis of evidence.

Place exam dates into your schedule

Final term/semester

Ensure your coursework is completed to high standards & in good time so there is adequate time to focus upon exam preparation.

Advance your exam preparation. Double time allocation for exam prep. Go through your notes compiled thus far - both course notes and exam prep notes. Add more quotations and references to your exam prep notes. Fine tune & advance your analysis. Practice answering exam questions from past papers. Discuss with peers and tutors.

Break before final term/semester

Stay fit and healthy

Maintain focus

Maintain motivation

Allocate adequate time each week such as a specific study session for exam preparation. Focus on what required of you in the exams and what areas you must address. Familiarise yourself with topics, issues, debates, analysis, quotations. Read from various sources of books ans and journals. Discuss your reading with peers and tutors.

Second term/semester

During break ensure you go over work from first term

First term

Whilst ascertaining course requirements, undertaking reading and coursework, ensure you have a clear picture as to exam dates, structure and requirements of examinations and begin preparations for exams (whether exams take place at end of first term or end of academic year). Obtain past papers, ensure your studies and your examination preparation compliment one another.

Start of academic year First term/semester

Whilst breakdown of academic year in this diagram is based upon the UK university organisation of three terms the basic princples on this diagram may be applied at comparative periods in the year to any university in any country.

© Farhat A. Hussain 2007

Dissertation/Report

Your dissertation (or report) will be written in the final year of your degree (in most cases) and will demonstrate your ability to conduct independent research of a given issue to a greater depth of detail and word length than previous academic work (assignments). Dissertations or reports are usually 10,000, 15,000 or 20,000 words.

Dissertations provide the means for students to demonstrate their academic level and ability and constitute a major part of any degree marking structure.

The skills required and developed during the course of your dissertation are invaluable for any post-graduate study and may be applied to a range of analytical activities in respect to your career.

You must ensure your dissertation proposal is sound in respect to chosen topic, methodology, organisation, structure, analysis and conclusions.

The design of your dissertation proposal is therefore an important consideration. Consult your course handbook for guidelines.

Ensure that you provide adequate thought and consideration as to your choice of subject, question and methodology for your dissertation well before you begin your work.

Liaise with your course tutor in respect to your choice of topic and commencement of your dissertation.

One of the major reasons why some students do not perform very well in their dissertations is due to late start of their dissertation and also a lack of a clear research topic/issue together with inadequate reading and lack of well argued work that does not pay sufficient reference to the literature.

Ensure you undertake a dissertation topic that is feasible.

Dissertation/Report: Research outline

Your dissertation (or report) must address particular academic criteria. Before you begin your dissertation you must produce a research outline which makes clear to you and your tutor what you wish to do and how you will undertake your dissertation in a manner that is reflective of academic research.

The research outline should comprise a core document of some 800-1,000 words and address the following (for an Arts based subject yet also applicable for some other subject areas):

Your chosen topic and question/hypothesis.
Your reasons for chosing this topic.

Present state of knowledge of your topic - literature review
-identify gaps in the literature and explain the research context of your dissertation. How will your work contribute to knowledge of the subject area you will deal with.

Why is the subject of your dissertation important?
What is your methodology?

What are the critical approaches that you will take in respect to the questions you will address?
-How will you undertake the dissertation?

Outline a breakdown of your suggested work into chapter headings.
What is your schedule/timetable?

What training/preparation will you require?
Will you face any ethical considerations?

What are your sources? Where are they?
-list a bibliography of books and journals you will use.
Obtain feedback from your tutor on your dissertation outline and adjust where required.

Writing your Dissertation/Report:

Dissertation Section	Do not start your dissertation too late **MAIN THRUST OF YOUR WORK** *Before you begin ensure you have a firm plan of your dissertation, also read extensively*
Title	Ensure you are clear of what your question and area of research is. You must adhere to the title and core hypothesis of your dissertation.
Abstract	An abstract of the aims, method, scope and main issues in your work should feature at the start of your work.
Introduction	Define the question. Identify key debates and issues. Undertake a literature review. State what you will do, also scope and method. Define key terms.
Corpus/main body of essay -Split into several key chapters	Engage in academic discussion of the subject of your work. Each chapter to deal with specific issue or area, taking reader through your work on a step-by-step systematic basis. Draw upon published works that are highly recognized and provide a critique of these works. Be conceptual, analytical, thought provoking, concise and provide intellectual argument. Provide draft chapters to your tutor for comments. Tutor's comments are essential and must serve to inform your dissertation. Provide ample evidence/data in each chapter. Analyse the evidence. What does the evidence demonstrate.

© Farhat A. Hussain 2007

	Ensure your work is well referenced throughout. Be aware of wordlength and time you have to complete your dissertation.
Conclusion	Summary of main points including analysis of evidence. What does your dissertation demonstrate of the topic/issues you have addressed? Ensure you answer the question/hypothesis of the dissertation. Are there ethical considerations or comments you wish to state?
Bibliography	Your bibliography must be comprehensive, comprise academic books and journals including most recent and also major works as well as other works.
Appendix	An appendix may comprise related additional data or illustrations that may help. Some dissertations require illustrations in corpus of work.
Presentation	Present and bind dissertation in the prescribed academic manner as outlined in your course handbook. Ensure your work is well referenced, bibliography is adequate. Edit your work before submission. Submit a draft and improve work.
Illustrations	Most dissertation topics are aided by illustrations. Ensure illustrations are of high standard and serve a useful purpose.

View dissertations in your university or department library so as to obtain a clear picture of topics, scope, style and standard of previous works that were acceptable to your university.

A dissertation or report provides students a unique opportunity to write of a particular topic/issue in detail and will serve as a major means through which your university and prospective employers will judge your academic ability. Select a topic that is of interest to you and is workable. Produce and adhere to an effective and realistic schedule for your dissertation work.

HEALTH

Whilst university studies are geared towards your intellectual development you must ensure that during the number of years you spend at university you preserve and enhance your physical health. Healthy lifestyle is a key to success in life including during your years at university. Adopting an active interest in (as opposed to ignoring your) physical health will serve you well during and well after your degree.

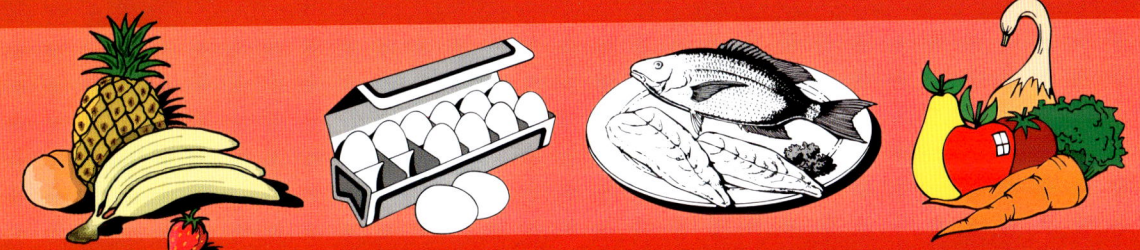

Eating healthy and nutritious food is essential for good health. Fatty and junk food must be avoided in order to ensure your body and mind are at their peak. Obesity, a serious yet also increasingly widely occurring problem in society, must be avoided through healthy and balanced diet (lots of vegetables, fruit, fish), and plenty of regular exercise (such as walking and sports) throughout the week. Smoking will destroy your health.

Enhancement of physical health will aid you in life and will serve to protect you from a range of health problems that may otherwise interfere with your studies, subsequent employment and life. When applying for employment your employer will wish to know of the status of your health in addition to your performance on your degree. It is your responsibility to ensure you are physically as well as mentally sound. Exercise that promotes cardiovascular activity is very conducive to health.

EXTRA-CURRICULAR ACTIVITIES

University provides a wealth of opportunity for your personal development. Extra-curricular activities such as sports and clubs will enable you to further develop yourself mentally and physically and will provide you very useful skills and ability (including stamina, endurance and discipline), opportunities and experience. Extra-curricular activities at university are also of use in employment in many cases. Employers are keen to know your personal interests/hobbies, your stamina and ability to work as part of a team and also what sort of person you are. Extra-curricular activities shed some light on the above and also provide satisfaction and happiness. Significantly you may attain valuable experience and insight into a given area during extra-curricular activities which may shape your decision in regard to your future. Shy not from a good range of extra-curricular activities which will present you with a challenging and varied week. However do not spend too much of your time on extra-curricular activities vis-á-vis your studies. Maintain focus and balance. Broaden your horizons and attain valuable insight, experience and development.

Avoid extra-curricular activities that are somewhat hazardous such as climbing Mount Everest.

Examples of extra-curricular activites (most universities cater for many dozens of extra-curricular activites):

Extra-curricular activities will build up your stamina and ability to manage your academic year. Extra-curricular activity also represents something of a challenge in regard to your time management and organisation skills.

The Environment

57 Enhancing Study Skills

We all have a responsibility towards the environment.

The environment is increasingly coming under strain as a result of negligence, over-consumption abuse and disregard.

During and after your studies:

Do not waste paper

Do not waste energy

Do not waste water

Consider using public transport to reduce carbon monoxide emissions

Visit nature parks

Plant a tree

Sponsor a part of a rain forest or an endangered species

Take an interest in the environment

Be informed
Be aware
Be alert

Take responsibility for the state of the planet

Massive demand upon the earth's resources by an ever growing human population is presenting serious challenges to the environment.

The 21st century will witness physical changes in climate, habitation and ecology due to the changing state (and degradation) of the environment.

Many species of animals (including fish and birds), plants and trees are under threat of extinction in the 21st century due to human activity.

During the period of your studies consider how you may aid in preserving the environment.

Using the internet, print media and television maintain an interest in environmental issues.

Fostering a respect for the environment is essential.

Saving energy and preventing waste of resources is essential.

During your studies you may also devise valuable ideas and practices to aid in preservation of the environment.

Careers that pertain to the environment are also valuable paths for the well being of our planet.

Farhat A. Hussain at Cambridge University

Farhat A. Hussain is an educationalist, historian, sociologist, archaeologist and explorer. He was born and brought up in England and was educated at the Universities of London, Exeter, Cambridge, Edinburgh, Manchester and Durham. Farhat A. Hussain holds various qualifications including degrees in History, Sociology, Educational Studies (various), International and European Politics and Archaeology (various). Farhat A. Hussain has also studied a range of specialist courses that include art history, history of science, technology and medicine, landscape archaeology, paleography and diplomatic and has also attained QTS from the School of Education, Exeter University where he has undertaken further courses in Educational Studies including in education management. He has received an unconditional offer from Oxford University for doctoral research aside from his research studies elsewhere. Amongst the specialist courses undertaken by Farhat A. Hussain in educational studies at the Institute of Education, University of London, are the Politics and Administration of Education, Education in Western Europe (distinction mark) and International Models of Knowledge. Whilst the bulk of his qualifications and work is in specialised history and archaeology, Farhat A. Hussain also writes and lectures in specialist areas of educational studies in order to contribute to the educational achievement of others. For much of the year Farhat A. Hussain is engaged in a number of specialist history and archaeology projects and the dissemination of knowledge in his specialist areas at both institutional level and in the public sphere worldwide.

Read academic journals and texts regularly in order to both attain knowledge and understanding of a subject or issue and in order to attain a greater insight and familiarisation with academic analysis. Enhance your ability in analysis by examining particular issues or subject matter. Analysis may be undertaken of a wide range of subject matter – even of a bowl of fruit. Consider a bowl of fruit (sit in front of a bowl of fruit). What does the bowl of fruit comprise? What does it contain? What colour, materials, textures are visible? What is not visible? What are you able to deduct in regard to the bowl that the fruit is placed within. Does the bowl remind you of anything else? If so why? What if any are the inter-relationships of the various elements within the bowl of fruit? What is the relationship between the bowl of fruit and its surroundings? Has the bowl of fruit made any particular impact upon you? Are you now hungry? Write down your analysis, illustrate your analysis and analyse your analysis before drawing your conclusions. The ability to analyse effectively is a most significant skill that is of the greatest value in studying at degree level and will also aid you very much in seeking, attaining and succeeding in subsequent employment. Your ability to analyse will be tested constantly in your degree studies and it is therefore essential that you consciously attain an understanding of what analysis is and how it is to be applied and to what ends. In academic studies analysis forms an essential element in the academic and intellectual process and it is upon analysis that conclusions are derived. The greater you are experienced in academic analysis the more successful your analytical skills will become provided you take the necessary steps. The accompanying chart in this publication provides some essential features of academic analysis.

It should be noted that at degree level all of your academic work will involve some level of analysis. You must not assume that only those questions that are posed to you in coursework and examination that includes the term 'analyse' requires analysis. All university studies require analysis on the part of the student. Often a handicap of academic work is the lack of understanding of key terms by students. You are unable to analyse effectively if you do not know the meaning of terms that are included in questions your department has set you or that you are reading in books or journals or are using in your writing. Do not hesitate to use a dictionary to ensure you fully understand the meaning of a term before you attempt analysis.

See also *intellectual development, problem solving.*

Problem solving

Further to the above, the following methodology may be helpful in academic problem solving (the term problem solving in the context that I use here is in reference to addressing an academic question/issue or problem) – a major element of study at university level which you must demonstrate proficiency in throughout the course of your degree. This section of this publication is intended to provide you an insight into the subject of problem solving.

It is imperative that you possess a clear and accurate understanding of what is required of you in regard to your coursework and exams questions. What are your aims in the task that you will undertake? You must thereafter consider carefully how you will achieve your aims. Be relevant to your task and ensure you provide yourself with adequate time to undertake your task. Do not exceed the time limit you are provided with to undertake your task. Rather than to attempt to address the problem or question in a brisk manner consider firstly the various options that you may adopt for your work before you proceed. Consult with peers (if at all possible), tutors and academic journals and books as part of the process of problem solving yet the task you will undertake is your responsibility. Whilst reference to the above stated sources will be helpful, you must also consider carefully what solutions to your task you are able to provide, taking sources into account and making use of journals and books for evidence and peers and tutors for guidance and suggestion respectively. In some tasks such as in examination you cannot consult with peers or your tutor and must come prepared yet your preparation for examinations can involve consultation with fellow students, tutors and most certainly reading from various books and journals.

Ensure that your own opinions are clearly distinct from the opinions of others (books or journal articles which must be referenced) when you conduct the writing of your work. In undertaking problem solving of a particular question or task write down the question/task. Consider what you are being asked carefully. Develop key ideas and how you wish to proceed. Consider a number of options (all to be listed on a sheet of paper) in order to attain perspective and in order to carry out your problem solving in a methodical and systematic manner, taking as much issues and perspective into account as possible.

Consider also how published academic work deals with problem solving in regard to particular cases or issues as a guide. Attendance at seminars will also aid in problem solving (one of the key reasons as to why seminars form part of the academic year). The manner by which you undertake your problem solving work must conform to high academic standards whose adherence to in regard to methodology and ultimately in regard to presentation will most certainly contribute to the success of your work.

Problem solving is an integral part of your academic work and represents a key manner through which you must demonstrate your intellectual and academic ability. Providing you undertake problem solving effectively and efficiently successful problem solving (practice/experience will aid you in this endeavour) will aid in your studies and in your future career. The ability to problem solve effectively and efficiently is a key skill that employers in most if not all professions seek and value in their staff. See also the 'effective analysis' section of this publication. Various parts of this publication (both text and illustrations are also relevant in regard to problem solving activity.

Reading skills

Ensure you know what to read and where to find what you have to read in regard to the library and also in regard to the correct place in the respective book/journal itself. Ensure that your approach to reading is characterised by focus, determination and discipline. Ensure that you do not depart from your required reading and begin to read topics or issues that are not related to what you are supposed to be dealing with in your reading for your coursework or examination preparation. You must be relevant and focused. Also think carefully of what you are reading and constantly build up a picture of both what the writer is arguing and stating and of the topic or issue you are dealing with on the whole. Challenge what you are reading and raise questions. Therefore be engaged as you read rather than passive. Ensure that you make notes and raise questions and issues as you make notes during your reading sessions. You may continue to make and expand your notes after you finish a particular reading session as you contemplate upon what you have read.

Approach a subject by reading from more than one source as this will aid you to attain a substantive insight and understanding of a subject than is the case if you depend upon one book or journal when dealing with a topic or issue. Take a break after a maximum of 40 minutes of reading. If you have problems concentrating in your reading, find a quiet place to read and read for a short amount of time such as 5 minutes at a time. Gradually build up your reading stamina by extending your reading time by increments of 5 minutes so that eventually you are able to concentrate in reading for at least 30 minutes or so before breaking.

If you cannot understand certain words do not shy from making use of a dictionary. In respect to your studies on the whole never shy away from consultation (with a dictionary or a person).

Use of the library and the internet

The library is a central resource that must play a central role in your studies at university. It is essential to consult the books and journals in the library as well as past papers of examinations that are often stored within the library. In order to gain the most from the resources stored in the library undertake a number of surveys of the various parts of the library so that you are aware of what is stored where. Exploring the library also will avail you the opportunity to 'stumble' across resources, including books that you otherwise may not have discovered and which may be of great use to your studies (including in fostering an interest in a particular topic area that you may later wish to consider for an optional course as part of your degree or for your dissertation/report. It is essential that you spend your time wisely (in and outside of the library). Obtain and read books and journals that are of use to your studies rather than to spend substantive amounts of time each week reading through books that may be interesting yet are not related to your studies.

The library is also a place where you may undertake your reading and writing. It sometimes helps to find a quiet spot from whence to undertake your work, if not a 'special place' such as a regular corner or place to work from. Ensure you are comfortable and well prepared for studies. It is helpful to work to a schedule and plan as to what you wish to achieve during your time in the library. Remain focussed on your work and do not be distracted. Concentration is essential for your studies and for those in the library around you who also are there to study.

Libraries also are places (in many cases) where internet resources are available. The internet is a prime source for information, including academic. Whilst surfing the web is always an interesting experience, it is essential that you focus on websites that will aid your studies. Visiting other sites for general interest does provide a welcome rest to studies yet must not be undertaken for the whole period you are online as your focus on your study tasks will suffer a setback due to loss of time and detraction of focus from your studies.

Whilst there are many interesting and useful websites on the internet for all subjects taught at university, and it is your responsibility to research on the world wide web to find useful sites, do not depend upon the internet for your studies in regard to coursework and certainly do not attempt to base assignments upon a particular site or piece of the work on the internet. Copying work from the internet is plagiarism which does not aid your development and may lead to serious academic consequences from your university (all forms of plagiarism - to take the work of others and present as one's own work - including from books, journals and the internet, must be avoided). You are at university to learn and must not engage in copying the work of others. Your work must be original in order to succeed in your studies and in life on the whole. You are however entitled to consult books, journals and the internet for information and for guidance and then to produce your own work based upon your readings and sources that must be adequately and accurately referenced and analysed.

Finally aside from your main university college library, there are other libraries that may be helpful and it is your responsibility to ascertain what and where these are and how you may gain access. The university library at Cambridge University and also that of Oxford University provide very significant book and journal resources as well as seating provision for their students as do all university libraries. Universities pride themselves on providing students a congenial and useful place for study in the form of the library. Some universities provide students a wide range of libraries to study within and use for book lending. Oxford and Cambridge students are able to make use of college libraries and those of respective departments (as is the case for a number of universities). For students of the University of London aside from the libraries of the respective colleges of this university, the University of London main library at Senate House (close to SOAS) is a fine library both in regard to books and a place to sit down in peace and quiet and in this latter respect often stands in contrast to the overcrowded libraries of many university of London colleges. All main libraries of universities across the world are of the greatest use for studying and it is up to students to be aware of what library facilities are available during the course of their degrees.

Libraries are places of study and must not be used as places for chatting. You must be respectful of those around you in a library and are able to chat elsewhere. Libraries are an excellent resource for study and a useful place to study and should play a central role in your studies.

Role of tutors

Your tutor is there to help you. You must ensure regular contact with your tutor. Do not hesitate to seek clarification from your course tutor as to that which you may not understand or that which may require further elaboration. Good contact with tutors throughout the year is useful in aiding your studies and in ensuring your tutor knows you and is familiar with your work. Your course lecturers will provide you the basic information of your respective courses whilst it is up to you to follow up the lectures and seminars with reading, coursework and examination preparation. Your course lecturers and tutors will guide you but will not read for the degree for you. You will also be assigned a tutor who plays the role of your degree supervisor. You must ensure that you are clearly aware of what is required of you for your degree studies and it your degree programme tutor (you should have a specific programme tutor assigned to you for each year of the degree) who is responsible for providing you with information of the course requirements and discussion of your work throughout the year. In some cases you may only see your programme tutor very rarely in the year for discussion of your progress yet you must take the initiative to have some regular contact even by email to ensure that you are aware of what you are expected to do and are undertaking your work successfully. You should also speak to your programme tutor as well as course lecturers for elaboration and advice on any given issue. Be courteous to your tutor and take seriously what advice your tutor has to offer you. As a matter of courtesy and propriety you must also take care to see your tutor during times your tutor has provided to see students or at a pre-arranged appointment to see you. Your tutor will be responsible for writing a reference of your work and ability and suitability for further studies or employment. This reference is as important to institutions and companies as your degree result.

Peer support

It is a matter of shouldering responsibility to help those in need whilst it is an act of humility to accept help when one is in need of help. Hence whilst each student is responsible for his/her own studies it is both ethical and practically useful to study a subject in association with a number of peers (your fellow students) for the purposes of supporting one another and aiding one another in the learning process.

A weekly get together (or twice weekly) enables a group of students (or a pair) to discuss the subject of study and to come to understand more about the subject and identify and thereafter address weak areas of understanding of a subject. More of a subject in regard to content is understood through collective discussion as the contribution by others, who may possess enhanced understanding and perspective, is a valuable educational aid in learning. The very action of discussion will also contribute to your communication skills and your writing should also take on the characteristic of academic discussion and therefore should benefit from greater discussion with your peers. Confidence of a subject also results from regular discussion and enhanced understanding of a subject that will also provide you greater means to engage in discussion in seminars and also in life on the whole. University studies should not represent a period of loneliness for a student. Loneliness is detrimental to studies and happiness and therefore peer support also serves to provide students the means to move through their degrees with others which is helpful for studies and for overall well being. Often students who feel alone during their studies on a degree course tend to take little interest in study time due to loneliness and lack of motivation to do well in studies, and this leads to a less impressive result at the end of the degree. It is therefore always useful to spend some time studying with others in addition to social gatherings with friends during the course of the degree. Studying with peers does not have to be undertaken with 'friends' but with others on the course. Choose a person or number of people who you feel will be well motivated and will contribute to your informal weekly study-discussion group and remain motivated and focused. What the latest films or television shows for that particular week are about is not what your focus in your study group should be about.

Further to lectures, seminars, personal reading and studying, study discussions with peers can enhance performance on a degree by substantively and may provide a much better result on the whole. Study with peers serves as an effective study tool that bridges the gap between attending lectures and seminars and also private study undertaken by the individual. Do not forget to make notes of useful points in the peer study sessions which should last at least 30-40 minutes each week. Discussion with a peer of a subject on the phone also may help as will email yet a face to face meeting is most effective. A special notebook for the purpose of the peer meeting is also a good idea.

Enhancing participation and performance and deriving benefit in seminars

The above activity of peer support discussion sessions and your preparatory work before a seminar such as reading and absorbing the most from lectures (see relevant heading in this work) will aid in enhancing participation and performance and deriving benefit in seminars.. Successful participation in a seminar involves a combination of preparatory reading and consideration of key issues to discuss (which must be noted onto paper) attentive listening and note making, participation via voicing your points (both those you have thought about prior to the seminar and those that have been raised in your mind during the seminar). Consider what you wish to say before speaking but do not hesitate to contribute. Often it takes several seminars to build up an established modus of contribution. As you are to pay attention to the discussion in a seminar, you must learn to streamline notes made during the seminar. Hence a form of shorthand or diagrammatic representation will be most effective in relation to time. You must not merely scribble your notes down onto paper as unreadable and unclear notes will not be of use to you later on. Write key words rather than elaborate sentences and make use of the seminars to build up your knowledge and also communication and organisational skills. If you are a dominating type person do allow others to participate in seminars whilst if you are a shy type person do participate in the seminar so that you are able to contribute to the discussion and may strengthen your understanding of a subject and communication skills.

Presentation skills

Undertaking study at university involves attaining knowledge and also skills. A key skill that you should learn to develop and make use of in your studies is that of presentation. Presentation skills are of great use on a university course at both undergraduate and postgraduate levels. Presentation skills are certainly important in many sectors of employment and some level of mastery or at least familiarisation and basic competence of presentation skills will be of the greatest use in seeking employment. Presentation itself is of the utmost importance by the time you are at university. Aside from your academic work it is to be expected that you are well presented in regard to your attire and behaviour. Personal presentation in regard to attire and demeanour is of importance well into your careers which will progress more successfully if your are considered to be a well presented person. Your presentation, in respect to attire and behaviour, will be one of the key issues that interviewers consider in reference to their decision to employ you. If several persons apply for a post for any given career and all possess the required qualification yet one person is not dressed well and is rather impolite clearly this person will not be successful in being granted employment. It is in any case quite important for one's self-dignity to be well dressed and well behaved.

Your written work must be presented to the highest standards and this involves writing in an academic manner making use of the full array of academic conventions such as references and bibliography. Academically acceptable presentation skills in writing may be obtained via browsing through published articles in journals and chapters in books and making use of this publication. Illustrations are also useful in supporting a piece of academic writing in the form of tables, charts, maps, images – depending of course upon the nature of your paper. Illustrations ought to be produced thoughtfully, so that they are relevant to your work and are not excessively time consuming in preparation though time well spent on illustrations will add to the marks you attain and will demonstrate your ability in understanding the topic of your work and your ability to present your work graphically as well as via text. Various software packages are available that are suited to the production of illustrations for your work. Illustrations produced in an organised, imaginative yet relevant manner are ideal whilst the use of an effective colour scheme is also helpful in demonstrating the issue of your illustration and your ability to present your work in an effective and creative manner to high standard.

Presentation of your work in seminar or to your tutor
During the course of the academic year you will be asked (for most degree courses) to present your work in a seminar and also to your tutor (in the form of a tutorial or supervision of your work). Organisational, communicative and presentation skills are of the utmost significance in the presentation of your work as is a sound understanding of the subject area of the topic you are to present. The aim of a seminar or of a tutorial is to demonstrate your level of competence for a given topic. You must read a number of works on your topic area in order to attain an understanding of what the major issues involved are. Your presentation must demonstrate that you understand the reading and the subject area overall. During your reading you should make notes of major issues that you are able to identify and include quotations of key issues by the authors of the works on your reading list (and indeed of other authors who may not be on the reading list yet whom you feel are able to contribute very well to the issue you are dealing with). Your presentation must be based around the question you have been set hence all your work must be relevant to the question or topic/issue concerned. Begin with an opening statement that makes clear what the issue or problems are before proceeding to address the issue via a set of systematic steps, which demonstrates effective methodology supported by evidence. Your discussion stage of the presentation must include a good discussion of the key issues involved including what your opinions are and why so. Your presentation should include an analysis of the discussion which should form the basis of your conclusion.

Body language
Ensure you are facing the audience and standing upright rather than swaying to either side. Do not fidget yet do feel free to move a little from one spot to another if it helps your presentation. Use your hands to help communicate your points yet do not sway your hands around too much. Be natural and do not stand too rigidly in front of your audience as though you are a soldier on guard duty. Smile and be pleasant.

Further points to consider in regard to oral presentation
• The presentation should take the above step-by-step approach into account. Your presentation may be undertaken via *PowerPoint*, overhead projector (OHP) and also via a handout that you may prepare for your tutor and peers.

• Each step of your presentation will be assessed by other students in the seminar and will certainly be moderated by your tutor hence you must ensure that every part of your presentation is relevant, justified, conducive to the presentation and also cohesive, well structured, balanced, well argued and accurate, making use of both oral and visual aids (see below). Speak clearly and at an adequate level of volume (no need to shout!).

• Timing is absolutely critical in any presentation as you will have a set time to undertake your presentation in. Practice of your presentation, including in relation to the amount of time that you have for the presentation is essential. Hence successful presentation is very much an integral part of your organisational as well as communication skills.

PowerPoint
PowerPoint is widely acknowledged and used as the major presentation tool on computer. The universal recognition that *PowerPoint* enjoys is due to a range of features that make this software package of the greatest value and usefulness for any presentation. *PowerPoint* enables one to render text and illustrations onto computer in a systematic and imaginative manner which in turn

may be projected (via connection to a projector) onto a screen for use in a presentation. Whilst the *PowerPoint* guide provides ample opportunity to familiarise oneself with the wide ranging function and facilities offered by *PowerPoint* we will consider here some key issues that need to be taken into account for a successful presentation using *PowerPoint*.

♦ Allow for ample time to design and produce your *PowerPoint* presentation.

♦ Be original and imaginative yet by all means browse through and make use of the sample templates that are available on *PowerPoint* and take into consideration presentations on *PowerPoint* you may have already viewed.

♦ Ensure that the design of your presentation (which may be firstly sketched on paper as a flow chart) succeeds in including the major elements of what you wish to present.

♦ The design of your presentation must comprise a very clear cut organisation that includes a cover 'slide' (term used to denote each page on *PowerPoint*) as well as contents page of what your presentation will feature, a good number of slides for the corpus of your presentation and a slide outlining your conclusion.

♦ Make use of large sized text.

♦ Do not include too much text on your slides.

♦ Do not merely read from your slides as this is considered very tacky and boring for your audience. Elaborate upon each slide as you go through your presentation. Have elaborated pages of your presentation available for your own use. This may help your presentation. However it is far more effective if you have mastery of your topic and do not need to rely too much on pieces of paper and instead use the basic information on the slide as your cue to elaborate further based upon your own knowledge of the topic or issue concerned.

♦ Do not use black text on a white background as this will not come across very robustly in presentation.

♦ Use a dark background (even if using a colour such as red or purple) and white or light coloured text.

♦ Make use of illustrations such as pictures and maps (some of which are available on the internet though you must check the issue of permission to use these illustrations with the provider/owner).

♦ The content of each slide should follow on very well and cohesively from the previous slide.

♦ Each slide should transfer to the next slide very smoothly (see animation) in terms of the visual presentation (like the frames of a film or animation).

♦ Ensure, as in the case of your essays and papers (and dissertation), that your presentation comprises academic discussion and make use of references.

• The conclusion must be hard hitting and concise, and based upon the evidence of the analysis of your discussion in your presentation.

• Use of sound and film may help your presentation though is not essential.

• Practice your presentation before hand so that you are familiar with each slide and the overall structure and rhythm as well as time.

• You must ensure that your presentation is timed well in reference to the time you will have to make your presentation and you must stick to your timed schedule as per your presentation plan which must recognise the significance of both content and also the amount of time you have. If your presentation is too long you may be asked to stop before you have finished and may be marked down for this. Hence apply good time management to your presentation.

• Do not shy away from asking your peers or others their opinion about your presentation before you present at your seminar and consider very well any feedback.

• A successful presentation will demonstrate competence of the subject (you may be asked questions by those in attendance) and provide a clear, concise, sharp and robust presentation making use of an effective colour scheme and illustrations where applicable. Do not forget to ensure your presentation comprises the essential elements of the subject you are presenting on (see various sections of this publication for guidance on research and presentation of work) so that your presentation is far more than a glorified piece of art work that may lack substance.

Overhead projector (OHP)
The use of transparencies on the OHP whilst now outdated is still used at universities across the United Kingdom and overseas. The essential points in regard to preparation and structure are quite similar to those listed above though in regard to transparencies these often comprise black text due to the background of the colourless acetate. Illustrations are useful for the OHP also whilst the issue of timing of the presentation is very much a major issue to consider in your planning and delivery of your presentation (as is practice to ensure that the presentation goes well and takes place within the time limit you have been afforded).

In regard to both *PowerPoint* and OHP presentations you must ensure that the projector (data or overhead), connection (for *PowerPoint*) are available. Also ensure that you have enough time to load your presentation (this may also be done directly by a key-pen for *PowerPoint*) before you begin and hence you may be well advised to seek to arrive in the seminar room or lecture theatre early.

Handouts
A key aid in a presentation is a handout. Producing a handout is not essential though a handout is useful for a number of reasons. Handouts provide the means through which those who attend and moderate your presentation are provided with a form of reference point. Handouts serve to reinforce your presentation. Handouts also provide evidence of your effort in compiling your presentation as well as foresight in seeking to provide those attending the presentation with the means to a continued reference point of your presentation.

Your handout should not be too lengthy or it may run the risk of not being read. An effective handout will be well conceptualised, relevant, well structured, well argued and well written. Use of illustrations is often useful where relevant. Referencing and providing a bibliography for your handout is essential as your handout is an academic piece of work. As an academic piece of work the rules governing the style of writing and content as well as structure of the handout are the same as those that govern your essays. In this respect devising and writing your handout provides ideal practice in your academic writing and may aid you in writing much more substantive pieces of work. However it is also useful to list major points in a handout as bullet points which comprise short sentences that offer very concise information of a point. Bullet points are very useful for clarity and space yet often are effective with an adequate introduction or accompanying text that provides satisfactory explanation of a topic or issue.

If you feel that there is not enough time in your presentation to cover every detail you would wish to address you may provide a good amount of detail in your handout and explain this aspect to your handout during your presentation. You may on the other hand produce a short and brief handout if you wish to provide a summary of your presentation to your audience. The length and indeed shape of the handout does depend upon your objectives. Pay attention to your choice of titles, subtitles, the manner by which you highlight your titles and present the contents of the handout. Page numbers are also vital.

Writing a handout provides you the means to take the initiative and therefore must be seized as a valuable opportunity that involves a range of skills from planning to completion.

Intellectual development

During your university studies as a consequence of your studies and indeed as a requirement for success at university you must demonstrate intellectual development. Indeed the assessment criteria for your studies in regard both to coursework and examination (and dissertation or report) seeks to identify if you have attained sufficient intellectual standard and level. Various aspects of intellectual activity are addressed throughout this publication. It must be understood that each activity in your studies from reading and writing to discussion and presentations by you must demonstrate good intellectual ability on your part. It is in this respect perhaps more than any other that university studies are marked out from pre-university studies (though arguably every level of your studies from early school studies will involve some level of intellectual activity yet not on the same level as that of university level) and certainly from writing and dealing with knowledge on a more casual and informal level. In order to ensure that you are able to write and communicate at a sufficient intellectual level you must dedicate adequate time and effort in reading a good deal of intellectual work such as academic books and journals and aside from attaining the knowledge that these publications contain, you must be able to absorb the intellectual discussion, and also come to an understanding of how the writers have conducted their research. You must be able to identity what constitutes the intellectual process and style involved in the books and journals you are reading in order to be better acquainted with the meaning of, style and content of intellectual work. Sound intellectual work comprises clear aims, methodology, analysis and conclusion, based upon evidence, taking into account a number of sources and applying critical analysis to the work of the sources consulted, which must be referenced in an academic manner, whilst the entire work must be based upon clear rationale. The arguments of your work must be rigorous and well founded whilst the writing style of your work must be elaborate as opposed to overly simplistic yet must also be concise, clear and coherent.

Concepts, Theories & Hypothesis

Concepts, theories and hypothesis are key and essential components of academia and will form a most central part of your academic work demonstrating your ability to engage in academic study in an intellectually sound manner. In this section of this work we will consider the nature of each of these three vital elements of academic study and intellectual activity.

Concept: An idea, in particular an idea that is abstract.

Theory: System of rules and/or procedures used to produce a result, also abstract reasoning or knowledge, also a set of hypothesis related by logical argument to explain, in general terms inter-related phenomenon.

Hypothesis: Suggested explanation for facts/phenomenon that are accepted to be true and authentic or used as basis for verification/basis for use in an argument.

Hypothetical: Thought to exist, having nature of a hypothesis.

It should be noted that whilst the above definitions are broadly speaking applicable to most subjects in some specialised subject areas the precise use of the above terms may vary from the above definitions provided - in which case it is essential to consult with texts that deal with your subject area. A further insight into theories follows:

Theories form a most central role in academic study irrespective of subject area and comprise the key strands of thought that have been developed for respective branches of subject areas by those who are considered competent in their area of specialisation. In scientific subjects as well as in mathematics theories form the basis for understanding particular phenomenon. In social sciences and art subjects such as economics or political theory theories provide a means to understand a particular branch of a subject. You will be expected to know and understand the major theories for your subject areas. You will also need to appreciate what key authorities in your subject areas state about theories and to demonstrate your competence and understanding of theories through their application to a particular issue of problem. You must apply academic criticism to theories where possible thereby demonstrating your understand of what a theory may prove or perhaps how a theory is ineffective/invalid, based upon a well thought out argument, supported with evidence that has been well analysed and whose conclusions are sound. Providing you are able to provide evidence and a coherent argument, you do not have to agree with a theory and may also contrast one theory with another for the same topic area. You will become more versed with a theory if you spend sufficient time analysing and understanding the respective theory. Reading the works of a number of authorities in books and journal articles of a theory and the subject matter of a respective theory deals with is most helpful from my experience with theories (both in studying and lecturing in reference to theories). It is advisable to also discuss theories with your tutor and with peers in order to generate further insight and familiarity with the theory concerned. Whilst those students who have studied a number of theories gradually become familiar with the scope of, and in some cases the nature of, theories it must be understood that each theory comprises its own properties and character and will interact vis-à-vis your subject area in its own particular manner. Hence each theory must be studied and understood based upon its own merits.

Examples of theories

- Political theory
- Economic theory
- Medical theory
- Scientific theory

A good way by which to understand a theory is to firstly seek to obtain a fairly specific definition of the theory concerned before moving onto more detailed reading. In order to achieve this useful introduction it is advisable to consult a concise book that deals with the respective theory by way of short introduction. Consulting a dictionary is also useful to begin with though you will also have to build up your knowledge on the theory concerned well beyond the scope of that offered in a dictionary for your university studies. Nevertheless for a basic introduction it is also useful to consult a dictionary including specialist academic dictionaries (such as a scientific or medical dictionary) as your first port of call. Theories not only constitute an essential element in university study but seeking to understand and apply them very much constitutes a vital part of intellectual competence in respect to your studies and requires an effective plan and study skills, an insight into which it is hoped has been provided in this section of this work by way of introduction.

Examination preparation

A successful degree will synthesise study undertaken during the duration of your course with exam preparation. In respect to your studies and also in regard to exam preparation do not spend too much time looking into areas that are not part of the coursework. You must make every effort to learn as much as possible about your degree subject yet this must not be undertaken in vain – that is to say excessive time should not be spent upon topics that do not configure very much in your formal degree studies. You must bear in mind how much time you have for your degree studies and focus upon the core areas of your course and not digress. As much as you are able to, select coursework that is relevant to exams. As you study a subject consider what the issues and arguments are and what you need to know in order to both understand the subject and what you may be asked in relation to examination. Therefore acquiring past examination papers and obtaining, from your course handbook and discussion from your tutor, of what is expected in the examination will be a very wise course of action from the start of each year of your degree. Indeed it is also a very good idea to obtain at the end of the year from your department, an idea of what you will cover in the next year so you may make some basic reading preparation. The more prepared you are for your course and exams the more successful you will be and the more apparent it will be to your tutor that you are serious about succeeding in your studies which will, in most cases, provide a chief means for your tutor to acknowledge your strengths – a notable issue in regard to the writing of a reference on your studies and abilities and suitability for further study or employment.

Some degrees comprise exams at the end of the year in which case you must prepare well in advance and not become complacent only to panic some weeks before the exams. Some degrees comprise exams throughout the year and requires continuous preparation and organisation of studies in light of key exam dates. Whilst being examined continuously may seem daunting it allows for students to focus for examination on key topics before moving on to subsequent work rather than to be examined once on all or most topics and depend upon high performance on one or two occasions per year. In the examination be clear to what the question is asking ensure your answer is relevant, based upon evidence and is well thought out. Prepare well for undertaking exams in respect to content and methodology required of you in examinations.

Examiners are after: Analysis and discussion with evidence and effective methodology, understanding of the main arguments and issues, what the main writers have stated, your views and an effective conclusion based upon the above. Work out your answers via plans and ensure you write well, in an academic format with clear arguments and conclusions that are supported with evidence. Valid comparisons made also are helpful (depending on the subject).

Preparing for a career whilst at university

Ensure you are aware of the various options that are available for one of a number of careers and ensure you are aware of what is needed to follow a particular career path. Thereafter work to ensure you have the required background for your career path. At university you must attain both knowledge and skills and abilities that will aid you for your career and this is what many companies and institutions are seeking – someone who is aware and able to carry out various tasks to a high standard and possesses the drive to succeed. Knowledge for knowledge sake is a fair enough approach for those so inclined yet never lose sight of the fact that you are at university to obtain a good degree that must be put to good use. Firms and institutions that accept applicants with degrees are after good results and people with initiative and a variety of skills and abilities.

Also visit and consult the careers people at your university and attend various careers fairs that are advertised. Attend careers fairs early in your degree so you obtain a picture of what careers are available and also begin to develop ideas. University should serve to widen your horizons. Be prepared to adjust your career choice if you find something more interesting and suitable whilst at university.

Successful study at home

Successful study involves effective studies at university and at home. Due to the workload that degree level studies involve it is essential that you ensure that you are able to undertake your studies effectively at home during evenings on weekdays and on weekends and break periods.

As you will spend a considerable amount of time studying at home you must ensure that you prepare your place of study at home in regard to organisation. A desk, chair and bookshelf are essential whilst a computer and printer are also necessary tools for students. A wall planner and notices in regard to studies help serve to perform both functional tasks (information) and aid to provide for a studious atmosphere. Conversely, distractions even in printed format on walls in your study area do not help. A clock is helpful. Ensure you are comfortable in your study area and ensure you are protected from causing injury to yourself whilst engaged in your study. Hence chairs with adequate spinal support are conducive to the amount of time you will be seated throughout the year and over the course of your degree. A wrist pad for your typing/key boarding and care taken by you in connection to how you are typing (straight arms as opposed to tilted/angled with as little pressure exerted onto the keys as will suffice) will also help prevent the development of health problems in subsequent years.

It is essential that you are comfortable and content in your place of study at home so that you may perform well with full concentration. For this reason it is not a good idea to study in front of a television (whilst switched on – unless you are reading for a degree in soap operas or film) or in the presence of your family and friends (who are not on your degree) as you attention will not be fully focused upon your studies.

Discipline yourself to study at home amidst potential distractions even if this means shutting yourself off from all else for 30-40 minute periods each day as it is the only way to progress in your studies. The most effective study plan undertaken at university can unravel at the seams if you are unable to conduct some form of study at home. As you spend much time at home you must work towards producing an effective study environment at home so that your study schedule and effort remains flowing and is not interrupted. Build up your studies at university, both in lectures and seminars and also in the library and further your studies at home. At home you are able to undertake further reading and tackle assignments and engage in exam preparation.

Ensure you keep copies of your coursework and studies (such as on a data key/CD) lest your computer crashes and your work is lost.

Reflection

You are also able to reflect upon your progress upon a daily and weekly basis. Identify areas of weakness in your studies and how you may address these areas of weakness. Reflection is an essential tool in order for you to advance. In order to address problem areas, develop a realistic yet effective action plan and shy not from discussing with peers. Reflection often takes place at home yet also may be undertaken throughout the day including in the university library and elsewhere (such as to and from university).

Dissertation (Reports)

Dissertations (referred to in some universities in some countries as reports) are normally undertaken in the final year of most Arts and Social Science degrees (and many other) and afford students the opportunity to focus upon a particular topic in greater depth than is possible through an essay. Dissertations are usually 10,000 or 12,000 words though in some cases may comprise 15,000 or 20,000 words. Ensure that your chosen topic is agreed upon by your tutor and that you take on a topic that you are able to complete satisfactorily. Chose a topic that interests you, that you feel is important and also that you are able to justify to your tutor (it may be a valuable area that very little has been written about). Do not undertake something that you cannot complete due to lack of/insufficient sources/evidence for this subject. You must be realistic about scope of your work in respect to what is practical and realistic in light of sources/data for your work and the amount of time you have. Your dissertation must address the question posed. You must therefore be relevant throughout your work and also highly analytical and critical. How you conduct your research in order to arrive at sound conclusions is of great significance for your attaining high marks and also in being able to gain the most from your research activity.

A central feature of the dissertation is hypothesis. A hypothesis is a suggested explanation for facts/phenomenon that are accepted to be true and authentic or used as basis for verification, also a basis for use in an argument. Your dissertation must be centred around a core question/issue/hypothesis which you must address throughout your dissertation. Your dissertation must be well structured and organised providing a clear and coherent framework of methodology. Your dissertation must provide evidence of your awareness of key issues and debates and what the literature for your subject areas – both in books and also in journals – states. Your ability to identify gaps in the literature and address a gap will form a valuable subject for a dissertation but must be workable in respect to your ability to produce evidence and data that your research will be based upon and must still draw upon published literature throughout your dissertation.

Dissertations are ideal in providing skills such as research and time management that are essential in postgraduate study and valuable in work and life. It is a good idea to obtain a copy of a completed dissertation in order to understand what is required of you and to also study how academic books are written and organised in order to guide your extended writing. Use of a full bibliography, glossary and appendix (where appropriate) and illustrations (where appropriate) should be made. See relevant illustration pages in this publication for further insight into dissertations, including research design and writing of dissertations. Your university department should provide you with guidelines as to what is expected in respect to dissertation/report. Timely discussion about dissertations/reports with your course or personal tutor is helpful.

Languages

The ability to speak more than one languages is a bonus in regard to study and employment. In the European Union (EU) the ability to speak French or German or another European language such as Spanish is an advantage whilst English is the major international language in the world today. Asian, Middle Eastern and African languages are also useful for research and employment especially if you wish to engage in work related to countries and regions in Asia or Africa or wish to apply to work at an international body such as the UN. Most universities offer students the opportunity to study languages in parallel to their degrees (or indeed as part of a formal degree course) via short courses of varying degrees of competence that are provided by language schools of the university. A number of private language schools are also present in many large cities whilst learning a language may also be undertaken in a range of other ways including via private tuition, purchase of a language book/CD/DVD package and via the internet. Private effort in learning a language is helpful in building up an insight and vocabulary of a language before undertaking a formal course. Certification of proficiency of a second language is useful when applying for a course or for employment hence undertaking language instruction at a language school is usually a wise investment of your time and resources if you must pay for the course.

The acquisition of even a basic competence in another language/languages is useful but only undertake a course in a foreign/second language if you have time and if so, chose a language that you find to be interesting and useful for you. Ensure you have some familiarisation of a language you wish to learn by reading through a language book for the respective language which will also aid you to build up your knowledge of the respective language and in so doing will prepare you for your language course. It should also be stated that university studies also provide students the means to improve their language skills in the English language (or which ever language the respective student is studying his/her degree in). University education provides a superb opportunity in respect to language and languages. In the global village that we reside in, knowledge of more than one language is useful and may aid your studies, research and future employment.

A lifestyle conducive to successful study

You are at university for a handful of years during which time you are full-time students. It is imperative that you ensure from your daily and overall schedule for the years you are at university that your studies are the major priority. A mere token activity in study each week will result in failure. In similar respect some hours of study each day combined with some hours of wasteful activity will also be counter productive as you may lose your way in your studies. Aside from the extended summer break you must be realistic and dedicate the bulk of your time during the duration of your degree to your studies so that you perform well and have built up the type of respectful relationship with your subject that you will require in order to be successful in your work for the rest of your lives.

By all means live happily and well yet as university students you must not lose sight of your studies and therefore you must sacrifice this time to ensure you achieve well so that your study effort is the major part of your lives at this time and is a continuously flowing effort for the duration of your studies. Do not allow yourselves to be distracted and do not waste time during this vital time in your lives (see also time management). Those who are able to succeed in their studies will be in a strong position to succeed in their careers not only due to good grades and therefore acceptance into good work posts but also in regard to the skills and organisation and management of time and priority all of which will be of great use in your professional work and lives.

Opportunities afforded by postgraduate study in relation to learning and career

Whilst a good undergraduate degree will suffice in providing you entry into a career, undergraduate students ought to consider from the start of their degrees the opportunities that postgraduate study provides for. Study at post-graduate level provides a much more in-depth and specialised knowledge base as well as enhanced research skills both of which are very useful in regard to a career at a senior level (often postgraduate studies work well in combination with experience following an undergraduate degree though this is not essential). It is often said that postgraduate degrees are for those who wish to teach at university. Whilst this is true, in many cases and teaching at university is in its own right a notable career path, it is also so that those who hold postgraduate qualifications are able to work in management positions, research and a range of areas. The experience provided by studying for a postgraduate degree at another university (as compared to the university where a student completed his/her undergraduate studies) also provides enhanced experience and background for a student.

Postgraduate study, whether in the form of a Master's or doctoral degree, provides a range of options and routes for a person and is something to consider during the course of your undergraduate degree. As postgraduate studies are specialised it is always a good idea during an undergraduate degree to consider what sort of branches of your subject area you find to be interesting and where you feel you can make a contribution vis-à-vis your subject area.

Career choices are always a matter for each individual to consider and adopt to his/her own taste, interest and satisfaction. Most universities have a careers advisory section and staff and annual careers fairs are useful. You may also access information about careers choices from the internet and from companies and institutions you may wish to apply to work for (also via the internet and via brochures from the respective company or institution). It is also useful to talk to someone who works in the area or areas that you are considering taking employment in so that you attain valuable insight.

Many study skills featured in this publication will also be of use at post-graduate level.

Resources and finance

Resources and finance is often a challenge for most at university and must be addressed.

- Manage your resources well and try to avoid debt.
- Work out (on paper) what your costs are and how you will address your costs on a weekly, monthly and annual basis.
- Prioritise the major requirements that you have.
- Do not waste resources on items and past times that will not be of use to you.
- A part time job is sometimes handy for resources and experience yet must not serve to detract from one's study in regard to time.
- Some financial aid programmes do exist and you ought to search these out in case they prove to be helpful.
- Being able to organise and address finance is part of university life and prepares you for challenges (including financial and organisational) in subsequent life.

It is quite normal for university students to face some form of financial dilemmas and hardship during study. However clearly university students of the United Kingdom and European Union (as well as many other industrial and developing countries) possess greater financial resources than university students in many poorer countries where both study and work following study are subject to major difficulties. Students in developing countries make do with what they have in respect to resources (which also includes improving the state of their finances, through part-time employment which is useful for experience as well as finance, and ensuring their money is well spent and not squandered) and in many cases do perform well. Hence everything is relative and therefore you must look on the bright side! Indeed, if practical, even after you complete your university education consider how you may aid university students in poor countries or indeed in your own country.

Respect for others

At university you will come across a larger number of teachers/tutors and students than in any other educational establishment you will have studied at thus far. Most universities comprise staff of hundreds if not thousands, and thousands if not tens of thousands of students (many from various parts of the world, various cultures and faiths and opinions) not to mention hundreds of thousands if not millions of books. You will inevitably through your reading and lectures and discussions come across a myriad of ideas. Irrespective of whether you agree with these ideas or not, it is essential and your responsibility to demonstrate maturity and mutual respect for others – persons you come into contact with, knowledge and opinions you come across in books and in the form of staff and fellow students. Demonstrating respect for others and the opinions of others is an essential part of attaining an education and succeeding in future studies, employment and life. University study provides a tremendous opportunity to come into contact with people of different backgrounds and opinions and hence is an opportunity to enrich oneself with the numerous advantages that diversity offers – an opportunity to be seized. A congenial conversation with someone from a far away part of the world will serve to enhance your horizons and make a new friend whilst also serving to welcome the person concerned. You may learn a great deal from this sort of interaction. It is also possible that as a result of such interaction your academic and overall horizons are very much enhanced and improved. Cocooning yourself with perhaps a small number of people for the duration of your studies will inhibit you from attaining the most from your time at university.

Conducting oneself with the utmost respect for others often serves to interest more people in communicating with you as well as serving to enhance your horizons and experiences. Respecting others including the opinions of others more often than not results in mutual respect from others towards you and your opinions. In your written work, even where academic criticism is applied by you to the views of others, you must conduct yourself within a respect manner. Conducting yourself with due respect to others must be undertaken during your studies (and in future life) as befitting an educated and respectful student and citizen (of your country and of the wider world).

Computer literacy

It is essential in the 21st century to be versed in computing at least at a basic level. Basic level computing literacy for university students comprises the ability to make use of computers for your research (using the internet), for producing assignments in respect to word processing, footnotes, bibliography, and also to be able to make use of computers for other basic tasks that include searches on your library computers for books and journals. The ability to use computer programs such as Excel (for spread sheets) and *PowerPoint* (for presentations) is also of benefit for many students. There are also a range of specialist programs for particular tasks and subject areas that you may find to be of the greatest use for your studies and future employment.

Whilst most university students are fairly computer literate, at least a basic level, it is useful to undergo a course in computing, and if possible a course that applies computing to your chosen course or career path (or something closely related). A course or training in computing at your university computer centre will serve to aid you in your time at university and may be relevant in your work after university and should be carefully considered. A qualification in computing will very much contribute to your formal educational background and may well place you in a better position to be employed (as will other supplementary courses in related areas). Employers are often keen to select those who possess more and demonstrate they are able to achieve more than those with average or a 'bare minimum' background.

As the internet is becoming more relevant to our daily lives the world over and is clearly of the greatest usefulness in respect to opportunities, including in respect to education and careers, it is essential that you consider and make full use of the internet whilst at university, including as a source of research for your studies. Many students who have adopted a keen interest in the internet, in respect to potential, have left university with this additional insight and applied their initiative and awareness in respect to the internet to creating services and companies via online with, in some cases, astounding success. The internet is also very useful in developing knowledge based services as is recognised and applied by *The Knowledge and Skills Foundation.*

International prospects

University students in all countries across the world must be aware that they now live in a global village where it is possible to inquire of and obtain employment in many parts of the world. Whilst students at university often take employment in their own countries many careers provide opportunity and prospects for employment both at home (country of a student) or overseas. Some time spent in employment overseas often serves to provide valuable insight and experience and will enhance the future employment prospects of an individual. For students of developing countries it is important to consider how to contribute to the development of your country. A substantive pay package in a developed and highly industrial country may interest most people yet the development of your own country through your work at home (country) will also be of the greatest value for the future of your country. Representing your country overseas through trade, business, diplomacy (if you join the diplomatic core of your country) provides ample opportunities overseas whilst serving the best interests of your country. In the present time some developing countries are facing a brain drain as many of their educated citizens seek employment elsewhere with negative consequences for the future of their own countries. Developing countries are in need of doctors, nurses, dentists, pharmacists, engineers, business people, teachers, economists, diplomats and professionals of other areas.

Sometimes it does help if graduates from developing countries take employment overseas where there are no local vacancies or in order to obtain valuable experience before returning to support the development of their own country. Students from developing countries must consider carefully where they wish to take up employment, for what period of duration and also the impact of their decision upon themselves and their country. If successful employment is gained by a student from a developing country it would be most wise to consider how to invest some resources and expertise and other forms of help to the developing country through initiatives undertaken by the respective person concerned. A medical doctor from a developing country for example who decides to work in Europe or Australia may consider how to aid in the development of health and provision of patient care and also medicines in his or her home country in the form of a sponsorship project perhaps in conjunction with a number of other doctors. Supporting the education of the future generation of professionals through school projects and other initiatives in developing countries is also useful and is an area that *The Knowledge and Skills Foundation* (including in respect to provision of books to pupils and students in developing countries) and other bodies are engaged in.

In respect to students in the European Union (EU), the European Union provides a range of Europe wide opportunities for citizens of member states including in education and employment. Most British universities cater for a good number of European students who are able to attend a British university for a term for their experience and knowledge base as part of their degree whilst British university students are also eligible to study for at a term in a European university. This particular route can be useful for experience and broadening horizons though you must make sure that this option is available and of actual benefit before opting for this experience. Language is also a key factor as not all European (aside from Britain) universities teach in English. Undertaking postgraduate study in a university in the EU may be helpful for a career if a specialist and highly rated course is found — hence seek and you may find. In similar respect the EU countries offer good prospects for employment and business and this is something that ought to be investigated.

A substantive number of citizens of the EU and other developing countries are sharing their expertise and skills in developing and less wealthy countries through taking employment with development programs and other bodies. Contributing to the development of people in less fortunate circumstances in developing countries through employment with a development project even for the duration of one or two years or two is virtuous, of the greatest help to those who will benefit from your support and will provide valuable experience to those who chose this path. Those who take up employment within the EU or other developed countries may still help those from developing and poorer countries through various initiatives such as education, financial and economic aid (better done through recognised charities and bodies such as the UN), provision of medicine and also expertise and skills (including in an advisory role).

A range of opportunities are available in regard to study and employment across the world. Think and plan well before you decide upon a particular choice in respect to career and location. In respect to working overseas, knowledge of local language and culture (even in places where communication at work may be conducted in English although the location concerned may not be an English speaking country as in the case of the work of an international body or company located in a non-English speaking country) will be useful.

The environment

Students at university should also consider their wider responsibilities in respect to civic responsibilities to society and as responsible citizens of the world in a range of areas including the environment. Environmental issues are a major area of concern in the world today and will become more so throughout the 21st century affecting many aspects of work and life as governments and international bodies attempt to address environmental issues and concerns. As the planet possesses a finite amount of natural resources the huge increase in population in the world in the 21st century will result in a serious strain upon natural resources that include fossil fuels yet also far more fundamentally, water and clean air. Fresh water must be conserved rather than squandered whilst fresh water in rivers and sea water is also under threat due to pollution by humans. The quality of air is also under threat due to the manner by which some industrial activity has been undertaken across the world. The use of such a huge number of cars/automobiles and aircraft in the skies has also contributed to the greenhouse effect by which carbon monoxide from millions of cars and thousands of aircraft has contributed to global warming as has the destruction of the world's rainforests (in particular the Amazon rainforest in South America). A range of human activities in respect to industry, carbon monoxide from cars and aircraft and also use of particular chemicals and substances in various types of appliances used in the home and at work have also made an impact upon the depletion of the ozone layer in the Earth's atmosphere which also may well be contributing to adverse temperatures and other knock on effects for life on Earth. Slight rises in temperature are resulting in the melting of glaciers and also the polar ice sheets which in turn may result in a rise in the ocean level in the 21st century which may cause wide-scale flooding of many coastal areas across the world and ultimately may result in changes to coast lines and the displacement of millions.

The habitat of many animals, plants, birds and fish is also being adversely affected due to human damage made to the environment - not only in respect to changes in weather and temperatures but also due to some very direct destruction of natural habitats. The destruction of forests by those seeking to make profit from the sale of trees without steps taken to plant new trees as in parts of south-east Asia and the Amazon region of South America is also a major problem. Some areas are undergoing deforestation in order for land to be cleared for developments and this also has contributed to damage to the environment and ecology. If we continue to lose so many trees in areas such as the Amazon in South America this will not only result in the destruction of many species of birds, animals, fish, trees, plants and insects but will also further accentuate global warming as these trees are needed to maintain the important balance that our planet (and life on our planet) requires.

Irrespective of the subject that you will be studying at university it is useful, prudent and responsible as a citizen of your society and of the world to take an interest in environmental issues and consider how at the local, regional and international level you may contribute to the environmental debate, concerns and action. At the very least you ought to consider how not to use too many natural resources and how not to harm the environment (and in so doing how to protect the environment). Information on environmental and ecological issues should be available at universities, including at the library and certainly so on the internet. Some universities may have a club or society that is focused on the environment and/or ecology. If not you may be interested to establish an environment/ecology club or society with the aim of learning and providing more information on this vital area that will affect us all in the 21st century. There are also a number of international organisations including the United Nations that provide updated information on issues pertaining to the environment and also initiatives that may be taken by us all to make our contribution to the well being of the Earth and all those who live on Earth.

It is possible that during your university studies you may wish to play a more active role in environmental issues or environmentally related issues in respect to your free time or indeed in regard to your future employment and career. Your time at university must be spent wisely in considering what role you wish to play in respect to the environment as well as your particular subject area whether you wish to work in environmental related areas or in other fields. It should be noted that due to increasing legislation in respect to the environment, many careers and also many aspects of life in the 21st century will almost certainly take the environment into account. Irrespective of which career path you do chose it is essential to be aware that we all have a role to play in caring for and protecting the environment and bequeathing to future generations a healthy and safe Earth.

Miscellaneous

University study involves a range of activities and areas, much of which have been addressed in this work. Whilst you must focus very much upon your studies during the course of your degree you must also ensure that you address all areas of importance in your lives that include personal, family and other/wider issues and responsibilities. Ensure that you live happy and balanced lives. Whilst at university the major activity that you will be engaged will be your studies yet you must not neglect other areas including your diet and well being.

Maintain physical fitness. Years of study could result in the build up of excessive body fat that will not aid you in regard to health and also your appearance. A certain level of physical exercise such as a daily walk/sport is recommended. Be active and avoid laziness. Maintain a healthy diet. Fresh fruit is more conducive when hungry during study than fatty foods. A range of issues including fitness, health and the environment are addressed in the illustration section of this work. It should also be stated emphatically that whilst university studies provide the opportunity to learn, not only of the subject of your degree, but also of the wider world and to attain new horizons, do not allow yourself to lose focus and perspective of your core aims. Maintain your focus. Your core subject area must remain your priority. In respect to your studies and your time on the whole do not allow yourself to gravitate to the fringes. University is a time to advance yourself for the betterment of yourself, your society and the wider world. Think and be positive. Succeed in your studies and in life.

Endnote

During the course of your degree consider the variety of areas that your subject entails and consider the possibilities of more specialised study and research at postgraduate level as well as the various openings that exists the world over in regard to your subject area. Ascertain what you need to do to succeed in goals that you may already have identified and provide scope to ascertain additional goals and openings during the course of the degree.

Time spent at university represents a privileged period in the life of most people. It is a time of great opportunity to learn and to build character, to develop knowledge and skills, to develop stamina and overall ability, to attain a greater insight into the wider world and to widen your horizons. Time spent at university is exciting, enjoyable and also very precious and must not be squandered. Never lose sight of why you are at university. In order to succeed in your chosen career path you must succeed in your university studies. Ensure that you are engaged for most of your time for the 3-6 years (depending upon your subject area – the writer of this work spent over ten years in university studies) that you are at university in intense, dedicated and effective study. Sustained effort and effective studying will enhance your success at university.

I wish you all success in your studies and future.

Farhat A. Hussain